Finding Faith
in the
Desert

Finding Faith
in the
Desert

An LDS military chaplain finds light
and hope among the U.S. soldiers and
Iraqi people amidst the challenges of
Operation Iraqi Freedom

by
Anthony W. Horton

spring creek
BOOK COMPANY
Provo, Utah

ISBN 13: 978-1-932898-19-4
ISBN 10: 1-932898-19-0
e. 2

Published by:
Spring Creek Book Company
P.O. Box 50355
Provo, Utah 84605-0355
www. springcreekbooks.com

Cover design © Spring Creek Book Company
Cover and interior design by Nicole Cunningham

Cover photos and interior photos courtesy of Anthony W. Horton
and used by permission

Printed in the United States of America
10 9 8 7 6 5 4 3 2 1
Printed on acid-free paper

Library of Congress Cataloging-in-Publication Data

Horton, Anthony W., 1957-
   Finding faith in the desert : spiritual lessons and insights from
Operation Iraqi
 Freedom / by Anthony W. Horton.
     p. cm.
   ISBN 1-932898-19-0 (pbk. : alk. paper)
   1. Iraq War, 2003--Religious aspects--Mormon Church.
2. Christian life--Mormon authors. 3. Meditations.   I. Title.
 BX8656.H67 2004
 956.7044'37--dc22
                        2004015447

DEDICATION

To my dear bride, Jeaneice, whom the Patriarch assured me would be a "strength and a blessing and a joy unto me." He told me well before I asked her to be my eternal companion that she "shall be a comfort unto your soul…"

The Patriarch was correct, and then some, as I have discovered that my sweetheart has been all of that, and so much more. It is to her unwavering dedication and steadfastness in Christ and her abundance of love and support for me that I dedicate this humble attempt of a book.

And to my first born, my dearest daughter Marah, who has taught me to love like I've never known. You have opened a new dimension of understanding, allowing me to experience how Father in Heaven loves me.

Words cannot do justice to the esteem and emotions I feel for you. Thank you, Marah, for choosing and allowing me to be your father.

CONTENTS

ABOUT THIS BOOK

As I participated in a sacrament meeting in the Coalition Provisional Authority Palace, the new central government building in Baghdad, Iraq, I was bombarded by several thoughts. To what extent did my understanding of the Word of the Lord influence my thoughts, feelings and behavior?

My mind reviewed the many years of study, prayer, and gospel lessons I had received, and a single thought began to materialize as I sat in the middle of a war zone. King Benjamin's words seemed to come to the front of my thoughts: "For the natural man is an enemy to God . . ."

I realized that war and all the horrors associated with it come from mankind's separation from God. We all face separation at times from loved ones, from community, and from country. The most difficult of all however, is that separation that happens when we withdraw ourselves from the Spirit of the Lord so that it has no place in us, to guide us along wisdom's path, that we may be blessed, prospered and preserved. (Mosiah 2:36)

It is my humble prayer that my stories and experiences among the people of Iraq will be of value to you in your personal life. The testimony of Christ is to be found everywhere, and is in everything, even in a blistering desert.

By sharing these experiences I hope others will find answers to issues they are facing in their lives. The pain of separation is not limited to the physical distance between two people, such as a couple separated by war. I have experienced extreme loneliness sitting right next to family and loved ones. However, I hope these stories can help bring a sense of peace and courage to those who read them. I believe we can find personal joy and happiness even amidst hardship, loss and sorrow.

I truly desire that somehow my experiences will add meaning and find application in your life, and bring you closer to the Father of us all.

— Anthony W. Horton

July 2004

CHAPTER ONE

"ADAM FELL THAT MEN MIGHT BE"

Adam fell that men might be; and men
are, that they might have joy.
—2 Nephi 2:25

The shock blast was tremendous! It rattled the Iraqi palace I was in from nearly four miles away. I walked over to the Tactical Operations Center for the Brigade to listen to the radio traffic. One of the most devastating suicide car bombs had just gone off at Check Point No. 1, also known as the Assassins Gate.

One of my companies was near the blast site, and I figured that many of my soldiers were injured. I rushed to the Combat Support Hospital, and sure enough, there were several soldiers being treated for wounds received in the blast.

I had expected to find several dead, but was surprised to discover that not one soldier died that morning as a result of the suicide bomber. One solder was standing directly in front of the vehicle as it was trying to run the checkpoint. When the blast went off, he was thrown backward nearly 30 feet, but he got up without a scratch.

There were enough explosives in the vehicle, however, to create a crater 10 feet deep and 30 feet wide. The rear axle of the destroyed truck landed right in front of my company's formation, about 400 yards away. There had been several Iraqis waiting in line to enter the Green Zone, a secure area consisting of most of the old regime's governmental buildings. These Iraqis were instantly vaporized by the blast. The truck that blew up had six Iraqis hitching a ride in the back of the vehicle. They too were gone.

Later that day I approached a soldier in the hospital who sat quietly, staring into space. Taking his hand in mine, I sat there beside him until he acknowledged my presence. His eyes were wet with tears as he turned to me and asked, "Why, Chaplain? Why does God allow such horrible things like this to happen?"

This soldier had spent the morning working at the checkpoint. He had been assigned to watch the Iraqis who were waiting to enter the Green Zone. One minute they were there—then suddenly they were gone. This soldier had shrapnel in his arms and torso, yet was more concerned at that moment about why God allows such terrible things to happen. Why indeed?

I cannot imagine what it must have been like for our first parents, Adam and Eve, as they were ushered out of the Garden of Eden—and out of the presence of our Father in Heaven. I know in my life, during moments when I have had an abundance of the Spirit, I have felt as though nothing in the world could go wrong. In contrast, when I have not had the Spirit with me, everything seemed to go wrong.

I have come to realize that ever since our first parents were shown their way out of the Garden, mankind's main struggle has been to reunite and reintegrate back into the presence of the Lord. After all, that is why they call Adam's transgression "the fall." Man became "fallen" or "separated" from the presence of God. Every prophet called of God has called us to reunite ourselves with the Lord by "turning our hearts to Him" and "coming unto Him."

My experiences in Iraq during Operation Iraqi Freedom have taught me that turning our hearts to Him is not as difficult as the adversary would have us believe. Learning to turn our hearts to Him is really to learn to live after the manner of happiness as taught by the prophet Nephi. He wrote, "And it came to pass that we lived after the manner of happiness." (2 Nephi 5:27)

My service in the Army has taken me all over the world, separating me from my wife, children, and the comfort and safety of home. I know firsthand the challenge of being separated from family while struggling to remain faithful to my testimony and covenants. I know how difficult it is to keep and maintain the Spirit while serving as a soldier in a far-away corner of the world.

It is ironic that in the midst of combat and intense emotional turmoil, the Spirit has comforted and instructed me as long as I prepared myself and remained focused on returning to the presence of the Lord. At those times, the Lord provided me with many opportunities to teach and assist others through sharing my personal witness of the Savior.

When soldiers experience the same traumatic conditions such as the explosion at the Assassins Gate, some will forever be traumatized. Others will be moderately affected by the ordeal, and a few will show little or no adverse affects at all. As a counselor, I have pondered this phenomenon on many occasions, especially as I have had to deal with soldiers that have participated in the daily struggle of the modern battlefield.

Where is the peace promised by the Savior? Then how does a person, after finding it, retain this peace continually?

Is there no balm in Gilead; is there no physician there? (Jeremiah 8:2 2) Where is the "rest unto our souls" promised by the Savior Himself? (Matthew 11:2 9)

Early one morning an LDS soldier came to my bedside. He said, "I need to talk, Chaplain, because I don't know what I should do." I could tell he was distraught. The stressful life in a combat zone had nearly become too much for him. After listening to his concerns, I asked him a few questions. "Are you spending much effort and time each day feasting upon the words of Christ? Are you working to be different than everyone else? Are you faithfully attending your weekly sacrament services and renewing your covenants with Him? Are your thoughts and emotions turning you toward Him, or are you denying Him?"

His head dropped, and a heavy sigh expressed that he wasn't living the way he knew he should. In an instant, he knew why he found himself so distant from the presence of the Lord. He was living a life of betrayal, which had separated him further from the Lord, leaving him alone and without the comfort and peace he so desperately needed.

Heavy tears fell from his eyes, and after a few moments, a new resolve entered his countenance, and I could see light flickering where moments before there had been darkness, uncertainty and doubt.

When we let our personal integrity slip, we diminish the light of Christ that is within us. This light illuminates the "way" we should live. Any gaps are filled by depression, anxiety, stress, misery, discontent, doubt and fear.

Another soldier approached me for counseling at a checkpoint in the heart of Baghdad. He had a great weight upon his shoulders. He had lost his peace and was struggling to find it again. His countenance was dark, but he finally decided to reach out for help. His story began with an extramarital affair. He had been in Korea for one year prior to being sent to Iraq, and like so many other soldiers, he had told himself, "What happens in Korea, stays in Korea." His only problem was that he could not seem to shake the memory of the acts he had committed in Korea. Guilt consumed him, and now he wanted me to pull a rabbit out of a hat by providing an easy solution that would give him peace.

As we talked, I was struck with the thought, "Just what percentage of faithfulness is required for you to be faithful?" This thought was powerful, and I felt I should share it with him, so I asked his opinion. His head bowed, and tears streamed down his face. He knew the answer, and at the same moment, also knew where he could find and reclaim his peace. It would come by keeping the Lord's commandments—one day at a time.

There are hundreds of choices we make daily that accumulate and affect our overall spiritual connection with the Lord. This process of separation is much like Velcro. When we hold two pieces of attached Velcro, many of us may choose to slowly tear the pieces apart. Fascinated with the apparent magic of the material, we work the pieces apart against their inherent clinging qualities.

Finally, however, with sufficient pull, we can completely separate both pieces from each other, leaving them to either remain apart or to be rejoined. So it is with us. If we are the ones doing the tearing apart, we must also be the ones putting the pieces back together.

Through such experiences with the wonderful young men of the U.S. Army, I feel that the Lord has given me insight and understanding beyond my worthiness to receive. I have been humbled as the scriptures have become clear to me, and I have seen things and learned lessons in stories and passages that I have never noticed before.

I have been able to share these insights with my fellow soldiers and also with the Iraqi people, as the Lord moves his work forward among His children.

GOING TO WAR

After the events of September 11, 2001, I spent more than a year preparing to deploy to the Middle East. Originally, I was to go to Turkey with the unit I was assigned to, but the trip to Turkey never materialized.

Our group waited many days for a boat containing our war equipment to return so we could shift our efforts to another location. So instead of being on the battlefield, I watched the initial combat of Operation Iraqi Freedom on television from inside the comfort of my home in Germany.

In a sense, I felt left out and unimportant, but my "hurrying up to wait" (an Army expression) paid off as I received a call in May 2003 telling me to pack my bags. I was going to Iraq with another unit, serving as a chaplain. I was excited and relieved all at once. The waiting was over, and I would join our good soldiers already serving in the War on Terrorism and the effort to rebuild Iraq.

I did manage to take two weeks of leave beforehand, and along with my family, I traveled to St. George, Utah, to visit my in-laws. St. George was a great place to go, since the dry heat there made the acclimation easier for me when I arrived in the incredibly hot weather of Baghdad.

The two weeks went by too fast, and the morning came for saying good-bye. I hugged my wife and kissed her, not wanting that moment to end. She felt so good in my arms, and all I wanted was to hold her and never let go. As with most of my deployments, the kids were still asleep.

We awakened them and I gave each child a hug and a kiss. Again, I wished the moment would never end.

Kids have a way of growing up so fast. One day they are into everything, trying your patience and tolerance, then the next day they are packing their bags to leave and go out on their own. I would miss yet another year of their lives. My oldest son was waiting to enter the Mission Training Center (MTC) in Provo, Utah. He had only just received his mission call a couple of days earlier to serve the Lord in the Durban, South Africa Mission.

I sadly realized I would miss taking him to the MTC, and thus miss a moment similar to what my dad and I experienced more than 27 years earlier when we embraced and cried together for the first and last time. I had not seen many emotions in my father growing up, and that moment in the Language Training Mission was a golden moment for me. I knew without doubt that he loved me and was proud of my efforts to grow up and be responsible.

I was so proud of my son's decision to serve the Lord and to give of himself, but inside I felt robbed and deprived. I wanted to share that moment with him, I wanted him to know that I love and cherish him. We spoke at length during those two weeks, and we both felt good that we would be out serving the Lord at the same time. My tour in Iraq was scheduled to last one year, and by the time I got home, he would only have a year left. Then his mother and I would travel to pick him up from his mission.

Tears were difficult to hold back. My dear wife did not even try, which made it more difficult for me. However, I managed to maintain the appearance of the tough soldier going to war. I finally allowed the tears to fall as I flew back to Germany.

This was not the first time I have had to say good-bye to

my family. In fact, I have been deployed more than 40 times in my 17 years in the Army. Leaving loved ones behind is not an easy thing, and I have found that no matter how many times I do it, it never grows easier. I have missed three Thanksgivings, two Christmases, and many birthdays. Somehow, it only grows more difficult. I look forward to a day when I will never have to say good-bye again, but somehow I know that such a day is a lifetime away.

I had to travel back to Germany so I could finalize some paperwork and deployment requirements for my new unit. The unit's soldiers had been in Iraq for over two months and were without a chaplain.

When I finally arrived in Iraq, it was 6:30 in the morning on July 19, 2003. Already, the temperature at the newly renamed and bustling Baghdad International Airport was over 100 degrees. I had left the cool climate of Wiesbaden, Germany only five hours earlier. The blazing temperature at that early hour hit me like an invisible hand, slapping me right across the face. Sweat poured off my body, soaking my uniform and making me very uncomfortable. It would take me more than a month to acclimate to the heat.

The unit I was newly assigned to, the 40th Engineer Battalion, belonged to the 1st Armored Division out of Germany. This was my first experience as part of a division. When I got on the ground, I was impressed at just how well established and organized the Division was.

Soon I worked my way to my unit, which was stationed in downtown Baghdad. I decided that the best way to adjust to the heat would be to get out and work with the soldiers. I spent every day out on the checkpoints, riding and talking with members of the unit. Unfortunately, I began to develop a body rash from the heavy body armor and the relentless heat. Outside temperatures would consistently reach over

140 degrees, and inside our body armor the temperature was much higher. Soldiers struggled just to stay hydrated and cool.

Despite my difficulties with the heat, I quickly settled into my assignment as a chaplain. Within three weeks of arriving in Iraq, I had already given several priesthood blessings. On one occasion, speaking to a fellow chaplain, I felt inspired to ask him if he wanted a blessing. His personal situation was putting a tremendous strain on him. I could sense his inner struggle with the Spirit. His reply was hesitant, but he finally nodded.

We found a quiet place, and I laid my hands on his head and began to speak. I was instantly humbled as I realized just how precious this young man was in the sight of the Lord. My eyes filled with tears of deep gratitude as I struggled to speak. I was in awe as I was allowed to see a small portion of the love and tender feelings the Lord has for my dear friend.

The tears that fell from my face somehow provided me with a healing and a strength that could not come any other way. They also provided me with an inner peace that came as I felt the presence and love of the Savior. This deployment has somehow been different than previous ones. I have sensed the Lord's hand more intensely and profoundly, and on many occasions, I could only sit back and watch in awe.

Soon afterward, an older and very experienced soldier sat in front of me, speaking with great emotion. He shared with me many problems that he faced with his wife and children. A divorce seemed to hang over his horizon, and he was at a point of tremendous loss. The tears were all too abundant and heavy. He couldn't hold them back. I watched this man—with two wars under his belt—cry like a baby.

However, when he was finished, he had a renewed sense of strength. Somehow, in the tears, he found an inner resolve and strength to change his attitude and be the man his wife needed him to be. At that moment, this soldier seemed to be more willing to change his previous attitudes toward his wife and their relationship.

Another similar experience came late one night when I was called to see a certain soldier who was depressed. As I listened to him, I felt a portion of the heavy burden he was carrying. In an instant, I saw a great young American sacrificing his life and dreams to be faithful to an oath he gave to support and defend the Constitution of the United States against all enemies, both foreign and domestic. Now he found himself in Iraq, a very hostile and unfriendly place for Americans.

He had endured the heat, discomfort, danger, and hectic schedule for more than six months, all while fighting loneliness and guilt for not being there for his wife and children. These things had more than taken their toll. Plus, he had just received a message from his wife that she was now living with someone else and wanted a divorce.

His world had crashed in around him. Tears fell from his red, swollen eyes. His whole body shook as he wept from the pain of loss and betrayal. I prayed fervently for help in understanding and clarity in vision. I wanted to see this young man as the Lord saw him. I watched as the healing tears fell, and his countenance began to change ever so slowly. The change that began to come about him was an inner calm filled with humility and meekness.

I felt a tremendous wave of love for this great young man, and noticed a change also beginning to take place within me. Somehow we connected in a spiritual way, communicating spirit to spirit. I can testify of the power and the tremendous healing that occurred during that night.

Chaplain Anthony W. Horton

My wife Jeaneice and I before my departure to Iraq.

*My first moments in Iraq. It is 6:30 a.m. and the
temperature is already over 110 degrees.*

Captain Weber and myself. I had arrived in the country with orders from my Stake President to find him and set him apart as a Serviceman's Group Leader. I had no idea where he was, but with the Lord's help I was able to accomplish my mission.

Here I am speaking to the men during a sacrament meeting in the Coalition Provisional Palace, one of Saddam Hussein's former residences.

Before I left Germany, I served on the Kaiserslautern Military Stake High Council. The Stake President had given me an assignment to find a certain soldier, Captain Weber, and set him apart as a Serviceman's Group Leader. I had no idea where this soldier was located, or what unit he was in. All I had was his name and an assignment from my Stake President.

I had turned to the Lord in humble prayer and asked for help and guidance on this matter, since the odds were stacked against me ever finding this soldier. I left the matter in the Lord's hands and simply went about my business.

On my third day in Iraq, I received an e-mail from a young captain named Janet Hall from California. She asked if I would help her find a soldier and give him a blessing. She said he was a good friend of hers, and she was concerned about him. Captain Hall provided me with his unit, address, phone number, and e-mail address. To my amazement, it was the same Captain Weber that my Stake President had assigned me to find!

At first, all I could do was stare at the screen as I experienced the impact of having my prayer answered so directly. I realized that my prayer wasn't the only one being answered. I thanked the Lord, then immediately went to work finding Captain Weber. Within the week, I had scheduled a time to meet with him and set him apart.

As it turned out, on the day we were to meet, I ran into my dear friend, Chaplain Helms, who is one of the finest LDS Chaplains. He assisted me in giving Captain Weber a blessing and in setting him apart in his calling.

We found a somewhat quiet place in the parking lot of the Baghdad International Airport. Behind my Hummer, we laid our hands on his head and exercised our priesthood, fulfilled our assignment, and acted as instruments in answering another soldier's prayer.

I felt truly blessed that day. Life could not get any better than that! It did not matter that I was living and working in a combat zone, where soldiers were dying every day. I was able to participate in the program of the Lord, and felt His presence in that humble setting. I wondered just how many other priesthood blessings had been given in that historically significant area just outside of Baghdad.

I have often thought about the events that fell into place to make that blessing happen. It was nearly unimaginable, given the lack of information I originally had, the size of the area I was in, and the number of American soldiers moving through the area—not to mention the restrictions imposed on us for safety's sake. But I have learned that when the Lord wants something to happen, it will happen.

I was so deeply grateful that I was allowed to participate in such a simple yet magnificent event to bless the life of one of His children, who, in turn would bless the lives of other servicemen in his area of operations. As my hands rested upon Captain Weber's head, my eyes watered, and down my face streamed the tears that allowed me to partake of the Bread of Life during those short moments. This experience filled me with greater resolve and determination to continue living in accordance with God's will. I felt true joy.

As I drove away from that scene, I marveled that such joy was possible on a battlefield in Iraq, so far away from my home and loved ones. My thoughts turned once again to Adam, our first father, and how he must have felt as he was ushered out of the presence of his Father. Did the Lord allow him also to experience and have such joy even amidst the seemingly extreme conditions of his separation? I believe He did, as Adam's heart was pure and held a great love for the Lord.

The unit I was newly assigned to was located in what we called the Green Zone, an area that included Saddam Hussein's palaces and other large fancy buildings. Hussein had spent millions of dollars on these buildings for himself and his inner circle, rather than feed his own people.

I actually lived in what was called the New Presidential Palace, which was built for Hussein's wife and daughters. I had left Germany expecting to live in a tent in the middle of the desert, but I was now living in luxury. Each day, I began to recognize and realize the many blessings that the Lord was providing to me. This assignment had promised to be a real exercise in patience and tolerance, but was actually turning out to be filled with great blessings of comfort and enjoyment.

One morning, as is my custom, I awoke at 5:00 and got up to check my e-mail and to study. I couldn't help overhearing a young female soldier in the main office talking to her husband on the phone. She was crying and obviously in despair. Something was wrong with her marriage. After about an hour, I checked back on her and she was still on the phone, crying and begging her husband to just listen to her and consider her feelings. She felt so far away and detached from her life and all that seemed to be normal. Somehow, this young soldier was going to have to find peace while living in a combat zone as part of a group of men and women all struggling to stay alive.

I have reflected on that scene several times. How similar that is to an experience I had more than fifteen years ago, when I was assigned to the Defense Language Institute in Monterey, California. I was only a Private First Class, living in an area that cost more for rent than I made in a month. I had to send my family to live with my mother in

New Mexico. I would stand outside at the pay phone for what seemed like an eternity trying to connect with my wife and kids. They seemed so far away, and I felt so powerless to affect or control our lives. I remember well my feelings of extreme loneliness and despair. How I wished my dear wife could understand and share in my experiences, but she could not. She had her own experiences to work through and understand. I would return to my room after speaking with my wife on the phone, and kneel down and pray for comfort.

Comfort didn't always come, though, and sometimes the pain was unbearable. I didn't understand it at the time, but both my wife and I were on the fast track to spiritual growth and development. I feel the Lord was personally teaching us, helping us prepare for tougher times ahead that would require longer and more demanding separations.

A young Lieutenant approached me in Iraq, greatly troubled by his situation. He was homesick, missing his fiancée, and very unhappy with the command's decision to give him a particular assignment. His career as well as his future was in question. He had serious doubts whether he had any future or not. Adding to his troubles was the fact that his fiancée had "cheated" on him and he was wrestling with daily bouts of depression.

With tears in his eyes, he sat across from me, broken and torn. His life was not turning out as he had planned. In fact, it was unraveling and coming apart.

After listening to his troubles, I suggested that he learn to pray and build a relationship with God. This only seemed to add to his troubles, since he didn't have a frame of reference from which to understand my comments. God was completely foreign to him.

Nothing I could offer him seemed to be of any benefit. In fact, the more I listened and watched, the more convinced I was that this young Lieutenant insisted on being miserable. The more he dwelt on his circumstances, the more he seemed to savor the pain and misery of it all.

I remember thinking about the statement the Lord made to the Prophet Joseph Smith:

> *And surely every man must repent or suffer, for I, God, am endless.*
>
> —Doctrine and Covenants 19:4

Repentance is all about changing from the person who acted or committed the violation of God's law to a person who integrates that law into his or her character and makes it a central part of their thoughts and desires. This in turn affects future behavior. Repentance is really about returning to and rejoining that which we tore or separated ourselves from in the first place.

I began to view repentance in a different light. No longer did I see it as something I had to do in order to be blessed with forgiveness, but something I had to do to eliminate suffering from my life, and to return to that heavenly presence I had separated myself from.

If I could learn to repent with real intent, sincerity, and a genuine heart, I could literally avoid a large amount of pain and suffering, and also feel the Lord's presence more abundantly in my life.

We are told that "Adam fell that men might be, and men are that they might have joy" (2 Nephi 2:25). Yet we suffer. Why is it so difficult to find joy amidst hardship and sorrow in life? How is it we struggle with our sorrows and suffer needlessly? We tend to look outward, searching for comfort in finding fault outside of ourselves for our unhappy or depressed condition.

That young Lieutenant never did find the peace he claimed he was searching for. He ended up developing a comfort zone around the issues he carried, but he never really found resolution, nor did he show any sign of wanting to have resolution. His demeanor and attitude continued to be somewhat negative and dark, all the while contradicting his verbal plea for relief. He grew cynical and pessimistic.

I watched as other officers began to avoid him. He verbally claimed he needed peace, but inwardly sought to hang on to his misery. He relished in it and refused to let it go, blaming others for his condition. My further attempts to revive his spirits and help him enjoy his situation had the appearance of being wasted.

However, over time I did develop a relationship with this young man. He felt uncomfortable being around me, and I noticed an effort on his part to avoid me, but I was persistent. I knew that the Lord loved him and truly wanted him to have joy and peace in his life. I would ask him regularly, "Why do you insist on being so miserable?"

He commented one day about being one who always saw the "glass" as being half empty. He then smiled and said, "I know, Chaplain. You are trying to get me to see it half full, but I prefer to see it half empty. Everybody has tried to get me to see it half full, but I just can't. I'm sorry."

Immediately I said, "No! You've missed my intent all together! I am trying to help you see the quality and workmanship of the glass, with its inherent beauty and the value it has for holding liquids. Half empty or half full is only a small element of the glass.

"What I want you to learn to recognize when you see the glass, regardless of the volume it contains, is first the value of it to you and to anyone who is dying of thirst and desperately needing to drink from it. What happens to the value of that glass at that moment? Is its worth not suddenly higher than when it is merely sitting in the cupboard collecting dust?"

We talked further and went much deeper, digging up several issues that he had carried around with him most of his life.

His real issue was not in the apparent separation of his girlfriend, but in his separation from God. He did admit to having spiritual promptings from time to time, which he had ignored and disregarded.

Why can't we just believe the Savior when He said, "Come unto me, and I will give you rest"? (Matt 11:28) I have noticed that believing in Him, and *believing* Him are two entirely different things, and while most people believe in Him, they don't necessarily believe Him.

The Lord wants us to gain experience and understanding, while learning to rely upon Him to take away our suffering and pain. He wants us to once again rest in His presence and ultimately become one with Him. He experienced sorrow during mortality, and so do we.

The only difference is that His suffering on our behalf offers us an opportunity to avoid suffering from sorrow in our lives altogether. The Savior lends us a chance to place in His good care our worries, our fears, and our suffering.

In this way, our sorrow becomes an experience of growth, drawing us ever closer to the Lord and His presence, integrating His attributes into our own character. He frees us from having to suffer if we will accept His invitation.

It is this freedom spoken of by the Savior that I wish to illustrate and share by offering my experiences and lessons learned through out my service as a husband, a father, a soldier, and an Army chaplain.

WHAT IS TRUTH?

In order to understand this freedom and the truth by which it comes, we must first understand what truth is. The Roman leader Pilate cynically asked Jesus Christ what truth was. In a revelation to Joseph Smith, the Lord illuminated our understanding of truth and the integral role it plays in our liberation from the sins, sorrows, and pains of the world.

> *And truth is knowledge of things as they are, and as they were, and as they are to come;*
> —Doctrine and Covenants 93:24

As a soldier, I have had to rely on a compass, instructions, and my training to get to an objective within the subscribed time without getting hurt, lost, or captured. I can remember always reaching a moment where I had no assurance, nor was I totally confident in my judgment, and I had to simply rely on faith alone.

> *Now faith is the substance (assurance) of things hoped for, the evidence of things not seen.*
> —Hebrews 11:1

In each case, knowing where I had come from, while knowing where I was, proved essential to knowing how to get to where I had to be. Sometimes however, you may not have a clue as to where you are. Once again, knowing where you began, and where you must go gives aid in discovering where you are at. Many of the soldiers I counsel know where they began, but somehow have lost their way, not knowing quite where they are at, and where they need to go.

I have heard more times than I can count, the proverbial response to the question, "What is the purpose of life?" The common response is, "I have no idea. You tell me what the purpose of life is."

Where are you in life, and where do you wish to go? To those that cannot answer these questions, the Lord has provided the answer, and has even built it into the fabric of our souls. They are fixed points in the so-called Global Positioning Systems of our hearts and minds.

One experience I had in finding my way occurred in Louisiana in the middle of a dark, starless night. We were being tested for our knowledge of nighttime land navigation. Our course was set in the middle of a heavily vegetated swamp. There were cotton-mouth snakes, brown recluse spiders, and just about every other imaginable man-biting creepy critter one can think of—all contained in the area where we were to go. The training area looked like a black hole, waiting to devour anyone dumb enough to enter it.

We were given our instructions and our time limit, then we were sent on our way. Wait-a-minute vines were everywhere, each reaching down like body magnets to grab clothing, weapons, and any exposed flesh, with big thorns ripping and tearing anything caught in it.

Out in the middle of this blackness that seemed to swallow life in general, and without the use of any light, I remember thinking more than once: "Maybe I should have gone left—or right—or maybe I missed the waypoint all together. You know, Horton, you do tend to veer to the left when you walk. Could you have veered too much?"

By retracing in my mind where I had originated from, I could determine my current position, which always enabled me to find where I had to go.

Of course, I said many prayers and had many thoughts of despair and uncertainty. Many times I simply stood still, consumed by the blackness of the forest I was in and listened. I searched for any sound that would lead me to believe I was either on or off track. But ultimately, I had to put one foot in front of the other and steadily make forward progress in order to reach my destination. But each step was made knowing where I started from, and where I currently was, enabling me to find where I needed to go.

Knowing truth liberates us, and frees those who feel enslaved and captive to vice, sin, emotions and unhealthy relationships. Living truthfully builds confidence and trust. We become more confident and more trustworthy as we become free from the consequences of sin and of separation from the Lord.

In one unit, we had a change of commanders. That particular line unit was the second one in the Army to have a female commander appointed to lead the soldiers to war if called upon to do so. We had a deployment coming up to Southwest Asia, and the training requirements and qualification standards were high.

After four grueling months of training and field exercises, it came time to be tested by an external source. Near the end of the evaluation, when everyone was tired and short-tempered, an emergency arose. A soldier in a battery located far to our north received a Red Cross message. He needed to be notified, but communications were down, and the unit hadn't checked in since moving to a new location. All we had were the grid coordinates of where they were supposed to be, according to the original order.

I looked on the map and determined that the battery was about thirty miles to our north. A debate then ensued on how we would locate and connect with that soldier. The executive officer had more important matters to deal with, since the evaluation were still ongoing. He argued that the message would have to wait until we got word as to where the unit actually was, while the commander argued that her soldier was not going to be neglected and forgotten.   I offered to personally deliver the message to the soldier. The executive officer laughed, then said, "Chaplain, you will get lost and then we'll have to send a detail out just to find you. It is bad enough that we have an entire battery lost. No! You stand fast and we'll take care of this."

However, the battalion commander said, "This chaplain is the only officer in this battalion that hasn't gotten lost. I have more confidence in his ability to find Charley Battery than most." Then she turned to me and with eyes of fire said, "DO NOT GET LOST!" She added softly, "Go find my soldier and comfort him."

I knew where I was, and had the grid coordinates that would put me within 1,000 yards of my target. I figured I could at least get to that point and then branch out and search for the unit if needed.

A night without the moon to illuminate the way makes for a very dark journey. I started out praying that I would be able to find the soldier. We traveled an hour following my compass, having to make continual adjustments since the dirt paths and roads didn't always follow the direction I needed to go. Finally I figured we were near the target location. We looked for the red light on the antennae mast of the Patriot battery, but we couldn't see anything. An inner sense told me that we were headed correctly, and that we should be right on top of the unit, but they were nowhere in sight.

I pulled the map back out and studied it closely. I then realized that the area we were in included a deep depression that could easily hide a unit. I was looking in the wrong place for the red light. After adjusting my search pattern and a few minutes of circling around, we came upon the unit, hidden in a depression, and not more than 300 yards from where I initially thought they were.

I radioed to the commander that we had found them, and that I would be returning shortly. I was struck with awe that I could be so connected in severe conditions that threatened to disconnect me and lead me astray, causing me to become lost and alone.

My life has been much like that experience. At times when things seem to be going so well, I wake up one day and realize that I am lost and alone, separated from the Lord and His Spirit. Then at other times, when adversity and turmoil are everywhere, I manage to stay connected to the Spirit.

Truth is liberating, and can serve to free us from suffering. It may not free us from pain or anguish, anxiety and discontent, but it most definitely can free us from the adverse consequences of making wrong choices and behaving contrary to our inner light.

One evening I was visiting one of the companies in my battalion. A newly promoted sergeant approached me and asked if I could spare some time to talk to him. We walked outside, and for more than two hours we stood and talked. "Chaplain," he began, "I do not know what to do." He had a heavy load of stuff on his mind, such as a marriage gone badly, accusations of wrongdoing, and the burden of the new responsibilities of being a new sergeant in a combat zone.

A full moon was rising, and the chill of the night began to bite at me, working its way into my perspiration-damp uniform under my flack vest.

I listened to him for a few moments, allowing him to not only explain his predicament, but to paint a vivid picture of his life so I could better understand what he was experiencing.

I told him that there is an unchanging truth connected to the situation he was in, and if he could align himself to stand firmly on that truth, he would find peace amidst the turmoil and difficulty he felt was consuming him. However, if he were to deviate even a small degree from the truth, he would experience anxiety, stress, and frustration according to the extent he had departed from that truth.

This soldier was losing sleep and not able to eat as a result of his situation. I found that much of his anxiety was self-created, and had nothing to do whatsoever with the truth.

The stress that was consuming him on the inside was the result of his separating himself from what his inner sense demanded of him. When he realized that there was really nothing to worry about, he was able to relax and breathe easier. Recognizing that he was standing on the side of truth made him feel more peaceful about his situation. Becoming free from the destructive nature of self-condemnation, this sergeant was able to see his situation more clearly without guilt, prejudice or anger. He experienced a liberating moment, and he thought I was the magician that had liberated him. Of course, I had nothing to do with it. I merely provided him with a new perspective, allowing him to see his situation differently. I was only a sounding board, allowing him to work through his confusion and inner chaos while providing him some genuine love and concern.

After a few moments of thinking, this sergeant broke down and began to cry. Embarrassed that he could be so weak as to lose control of his emotions, he struggled to fight the tears back, but gave in eventually as he needed to cry. With my arm around him, we stood together in the moonlight, in a combat zone on guard duty. The tears ran their course, but not before applying the medicinal magic that tears are capable of doing. Somehow much of his stress was gone, and he was more inclined to accept the truth of his situation. He claimed the thing that hurt him the most was that while he stood guard in Baghdad, at the point of his nation's spear, being faithful to not only his obligation to the military, but also to his wife and children, she had abandoned him, and had done so with great anger and bitterness. He was dealing with abandonment and disloyalty issues, which had grown to the point of affecting his sleep and eating habits. And suddenly, for the first time he was able to find peace in all of it.

As I stood and listened to him, I was immensely grateful that I had a wife that has integrity and is loyal. I was grateful that I did not have to feel abandoned, as this soldier was feeling. I was deeply grateful for truth, and for my testimony of a living God, and for the knowledge and testimony that the Savior's sacrifice has opened the way for me so I do not have to suffer. I may have to encounter the troubles and difficulties of life, but I do not have to suffer! The Lord has promised this, leaving that choice with us.

> For behold, I, God, have suffered these things for all, that they might not suffer if they would repent;
>
> But if they would not repent they must suffer even as I;
> —Doctrine and Covenants 19:16-17

THE FALL

Language has always fascinated me. We say, "I fell, and need to get back up," to describe a condition caused by a bad choice or series of bad choices. The alcoholic will use the term "fall" to describe returning to alcohol after a period of resisting the addiction. A popular television commercial once showed an elderly woman falling backward. After an unsuccessful struggle to get back up, she exclaimed, "Help me! I've fallen, and I can't get up."

Culturally, we use the term "fall" to highlight our failures or misfortunes. What we are really saying when we indicate that we have fallen is that we have separated ourselves from something. Many times the separation that takes place physically is preceded by a spiritual separation.

Theologically the word "fall" is most always associated with Adam and Eve "falling" from the presence of God, and the impact that their separation from God has had on the rest of the human race.

Many of the difficulties we face in life are the result of separation of one kind or another and the degree to which we suffer affects not only ourselves but also those around us. In perhaps the greatest separation of all time, our first parents were ushered out of the presence of God, affecting every man and woman yet to follow. The model for our first parents was the model of our Heavenly Parents, who coached and encouraged Adam and Eve until the day came for them to leave.

Imagine the devastating effects of being ushered out of Heavenly Father's presence! I have often pondered that moment in time when Adam's heart must have been filled with despair and anguish. In ushering our first parents out of His presence, the Lord was kind and understanding to the needs of Adam and Eve, giving them sufficient instruction on how to live and survive outside of the Garden of Eden. The Lord gave Adam and Eve instructions on what to eat. No longer were they able to freely partake of the fruit of the Garden. They had to find their nourishment in the herb of the field, after toiling long and hard for it.

Adam surely suffered great despair and anxiety. The Lord promised Adam however, "In the sweat of thy face shalt thou eat bread..." (Gen 2:19) No longer would he be able to freely eat of the "fruit," which represented the love of God, that was so abundant in the Garden. Herbs of the field would be his source of nourishment from that moment on. However, a loving and compassionate Heavenly Father would not utterly abandon Adam. The sweet feelings that Adam had grown so accustomed to in the garden—the Bread of Life—would be his to partake of again, through tears of remorse and repentance. Adam knew that hard work, commitment and humility are crucial ingredients to a happy life. He would now have to live up to the charge given to him in the premortal existence—to overcome and subdue the flesh and the world. (Gen 1:28)

I have served in the Army for nearly two decades, with experience in a broad area of service. Enlisting in 1987, I have learned what it is like to maintain my testimony amid turmoil, chaos, and temptation of just about every kind. As an officer, I've learned how to not only maintain my testimony, but how to lead others by setting the right example. As a chaplain, I've been reintroduced to the struggles the enlisted soldiers endure, as well as the leadership issues that officers face daily. I have served in the United States and on foreign soil, in peacetime as well as in wartime. I have lived in and operated in the combat fields of Kuwait, Kosovo, and Iraq, and served both soldiers and the people there, helping them to understand and live freely. I have been separated from my wife and children the better portion of the time I have been married.

Separation is an issue I've had ample time to contemplate and understand. It is an issue that affects every one of us, whether we are in the safety of our own homes, or struggling along without friends and loved ones. The scriptures are full of examples of how to deal with separation, and how to help others experiencing the same.

It is the result of certain events happening in my life

*I am standing next to a giant monument of Saddam Hussein
that had been removed from the top of a nearby palace.*

My assistant William Sturm and myself stand with an Iraqi woman inside of the Coalition headquarters' chapel, which was once a large ballroom. This young lady is an Assyrian Catholic. She isn't of Arab descent, but Assyrian, and thus one of the native Iraqis. She attended several of our services, and received a Book of Mormon in Arabic.

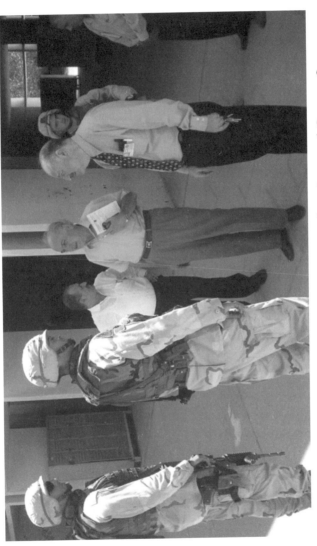

Lieutenant Colonel Coats, commander of the 40th Engineer Battalion, and Captain Brown, a company commander, discuss some building repairs with members of the Baghdad University Engineering Department. The department dean is the man on the right wearing a tie. After a tour of the school, we went back to the dean's office, where they offered us a drink of tea. I declined, and the dean asked me, "Why not? Are you a Mormon?" It turned out that he had attended the University of Utah, and became friends with several LDS people there...

It is clear to see that this soldier is feeling down. The separation from loved ones, constant danger, incredible heat and constant battle missions have a way of wearing down individuals who lack faith. One of my key duties in Iraq was to build up the faith of the soldiers and bring them closer to Heavenly Father.

that has brought me to this task of writing my thoughts and feelings down surrounding what I believe to be the most important lesson I have learned so far. I will never forget that emotional moment when I was to board a plane to go away for two months to basic training.

Standing at the Salt Lake Airport, it came time for me to board. My wife and oldest daughter began crying uncontrollably, and getting on that airplane was one of the most difficult things I have ever had to do. I can still hear Marah, a five-year-old at the time, catching the attention of everyone present by yelling, "Oh Daddy, don't leave us alone. Daddy, I don't want you to go!"

I couldn't control my emotions as I tore myself from their embrace and began to turn toward the door leading to the plane. This scene also affected others in the waiting area. Later, an older couple approached me on the aircraft and lovingly told me that my family and I would be in their prayers.

How alone I felt on that plane ride that would ultimately take me to Fort Dix, New Jersey. I sensed no other source of comfort could ever satisfy my pain of separation and loneliness for my family, except for the love and comfort of the Savior. I prayed hard for comfort, and it came amidst the tears of humility with a broken heart and a very contrite spirit. The assurance and the peace that was given me in my time of desperate need strengthened my testimony, and helped to prepare me for more difficult separations to come.

A thought struck me one day while discussing religion with another chaplain friend of mine. Chaplain Brian Reck and I attended the Chaplain Officer Basic Course together, and we have been blessed to be able to work close together in Baghdad. Chaplain Reck is also an LDS chaplain, and has provided me with important fellowship and friendship amidst the challenges of ministering in a combat environment. My Chaplain Assistant was there listening to our discussion, and he interrupted us to ask what Mormons believed concerning grace and works. Naturally, this was a loaded question, and I knew that the question was leading us to more than a mere discussion.

As Chaplain Reck began to answer, I sat and listened, wishing I had a way of demonstrating to people who ask such questions the error of their ways. As I sat listening and pondering, I suddenly recognized a truth I had never seen before. Adam did fall, and he fell that we might be, and in our being, we are offered joy. But we must choose the joy offered us in order to receive it, and in our choosing, we must become different toward others and ourselves. It is this new way of being that I believe answers the first and greatest of all commandments: to truly love our neighbor as ourselves, we must first learn to love God with all our being, or all that we are.

My assistant was trying to point out by using the Bible that Grace is all that is needed for a person to be saved. "You Mormons," he said, "have added to the word by saying that you have to work your way into heaven. I am saved because I have accepted Jesus Christ as my personal Lord and Savior and it is by His grace alone that I am saved."

Truth is unchanging, the same today as it was yesterday, and as it will be throughout eternity. God cannot change—not today, yesterday or tomorrow. Therefore, if all we have to do today is to make a proclamation and then say we believe, what about the sins we commit after that moment? The general consensus in Christendom is that once you are saved, you cannot fall, because the redeeming blood of the Christ paid that price in full.

If this were true, then why did Adam fall? Wasn't he saved in the Garden of Eden, knowing God and partaking of His fruit freely? How is it Adam fell for simply eating a fruit that was forbidden, while men today can do much worse, but be forgiven by simply proclaiming Christ as their personal Savior?

The fall of Adam is a principle that is still in affect today just as it was in Adam's day. We can fall as many times as we can get back up, or perhaps more accurately, we can separate ourselves from God's presence by choice regardless of what we proclaim or what He has done for us. The choice is ours. Adam's fall separated him from not only the physical presence of the Lord, but also His spiritual presence. After being cast out physically, Adam was provided a way to reconnect or reunite spiritually, enabling him to enjoy life on earth.

THE PROBLEM IS NEVER THE PROBLEM!

Someone once wisely said, "The problem is never the problem! The problem is how you see the problem. Change how you see the problem and what you called the problem goes away."

Before I arrived in Germany, one of the Chaplains conducting the worship services at the airbase I was assigned to actually stood at the pulpit every Sunday and preached anti-Mormon material. In his bulletins he would print the material he had preached about, all of it being an attempt to safeguard his little flock from me—the "wolf in sheep's clothing." Until this assignment, I had never experienced such open and flagrant disregard to the Army Chaplaincy's Pluralistic policy on Religious Support.

After a few weeks of not being allowed to participate in the Sunday services, I was given the assignment to assist one Sunday by simply reading a verse of scripture from the

New Testament. As I got up to read the verse, the entire congregation of soldiers got up and walked out of the Chapel to protest my participation. They then lingered outside the Chapel, continuing their protest.

It was a personal slap in the face. They intentionally wanted to hurt and embarrass me. Their intent was to run me out of the Army, since they believed in their hearts that I did not belong. One gentleman who organized the protest later called me and told me he was appalled that the Army would allow a Mormon to be a chaplain. He wanted me to give him a point of contact to whom he could further protest my assignment.

I prayed with all of my soul to see those people as the Lord saw them. I desperately needed to know what the Lord wanted me to do, rather than do what I wanted to do. I knew if I did what I felt like doing, I would have made the problem much worse.

My natural eyes saw a very big problem. I was stuck in a place where the people were hostile toward me and my religious beliefs. As I dwelt upon this apparent problem, I was struck with the thought that perhaps the Lord saw no problem at all, but rather saw an opportunity. Perhaps that very opportunity was arranged and provided by the Lord Himself, and why did I see it as a problem? My perception changed somewhat. I was humbled, and as I began to work through the situation, I moved forward slowly and with much prayer. Hearts soon softened, and people changed. Within a short period of time, nearly everyone that had walked out on me in protest became some of my most dedicated friends, faithfully attending every service where I preached. Many came to listen not to the sermons I preached, but to hear the humble testimony I shared with each sermon. They felt and enjoyed the Spirit of the Lord, which fed them and edified them.

Many of them repeatedly begged my forgiveness for having been so un-Christian and so quick to judge. When I received orders to report to Iraq, many of those people that had walked out in protest now shed tears of remorse and sadness for losing me. I had learned a lesson I will not soon forget: the problem really never is the problem! The real problem we have in life is how we see our so-called problems. When we learn to see things as the Lord does, somehow our supposed problems go away, leaving an opportunity for us to let our light shine, and to touch the lives of others.

ALL THINGS POINT TO CHRIST

All we have to do is look!

My good mother, along with dedicated primary teachers, taught me that "all things point to Christ." I have to admit that I have tried to validate this instruction all of my life, especially where the Old Testament is concerned. There are simply some things written in that book that I have had real difficulty in finding any correlation to Christ.

I have learned however, that my mother and church teachers were correct. All things do point to Christ, and the real fun and excitement is to be found in the search. I add my personal witness of this fact by relating scriptures and life experiences. I suspect there will be those that will argue that not all things testify of the Christ, and they will ask how such things as adversity, hardship, and suffering point to Christ, or, how pornography and other such vices point to Christ.

Does the actual sin point to Christ? Of course it doesn't, but there is a line moving directly opposite to the line that a person traverses while sinning, a reciprocal line that is a direct line back to the Savior. In the moment that we separate ourselves from the Spirit of the Lord, we travel in a straight line directly away from the Lord. By turning ourselves completely around, we return to the Lord.

A person acquainted with mountaineering or land navigation will understand that in order to find a destination, sometimes you need to rely on knowing accurately where the starting point is. Anyone with any experience with a compass and map will say that knowing where you started— and knowing where you are—will greatly aid in discovering where you want to go.

Those individuals who have gotten caught up in any vice that leads the soul away from Christ will also create a new starting point. Addiction, sin, and anything else that leads people away from the Savior will cause them to become lost. How do we find our way out of the thicket and mire? Simple deduction will immediately reveal that all is not lost. By closely examining the terrain and destination, a person can determine the proper path back to the Lord.

The thicket and mire may be difficult to traverse, but the Light of Christ illuminates and leads our way, and the Holy Ghost testifies of it. The question people face is, "How badly do I want to change my heart, mind, and soul in order to become free from the grasp of sin?"

As a chaplain in the United States Army, I have the opportunity daily to read, pray, and discuss life's most important issues with soldiers from all walks of life. I have learned from them that what really matters most is a sense of belonging to a family, and in some way being connected to God. It never fails to amaze me just how integral this theme is to all of us.

One experience that illustrates this principle occurred somewhere in the desert in the middle of Kuwait. I had met a Kuwaiti by the name of Sudan, who invited a small group of soldiers and myself to eat dinner at his tent, located several miles into the desert. This was a tremendous opportunity for these American soldiers to experience the traditions and culture of the people they were defending. It was nearly midnight before we got to eat, but for roughly four hours I found myself locked in a conversation about religion with Sudan and a few of his so-called neighbors. (We never saw the neighbors' tents, but we assumed that they were somewhere over the dunes on the horizon.)

Sudan taught me more in those few hours about his people and their beliefs than I've learned in all of my studies. One of the most startling discoveries was that even in the barren deserts of Kuwait and Saudi Arabia, humble people live and practice according to the religious beliefs given to Abraham, and then handed down to Ishmael. I learned to focus not on our major religious differences, but rather on the similarities and overlapping likenesses that testified to me of Christ and His unchanging gospel plan. The Lord has provided ways for all of us to partake of His unwavering and perfect love.

Another humbling experience that had a great impact on me happened a few years ago in the desert of North Fort Bliss, Texas, as my unit was undergoing a strenuous evaluation by a unit assigned to judge our readiness to go to war. We were in the field, going nonstop for more than three weeks, working hard and doing everything that might be required of us in a combat situation.

One soldier, a returned missionary, approached me and asked if I could give him a blessing. He looked tired and worn out. More than that, he looked like he was in a serious battle with the adversary and losing ground. We talked a few moments, and he indicated that he was struggling and hurting inside. He needed to feel that the Lord still loved him. We walked out into the desert and under the clouds of a wintry afternoon I laid my hands on his head and gave him a blessing. In the instant that my hands touched his head, I was filled with a rush of tremendous emotions—of love and affection that the Lord held for him. I could not speak for a few moments for the torrent of emotion I felt. As I gained control of my ability to speak, I began the blessing by assuring the young man just how precious he was to the Lord, and how fortunate he was to have the testimony of the Savior. I assured him that the Lord had heard his humble prayers and this was His answer.

After that blessing, the soldier and I embraced, and he walked away, leaving me to ponder the events that had just transpired. The appearance was that he needed a blessing and came to me for one, but the reality was I so desperately needed to be blessed of him and his personal love and devotion to the Lord.

A FALLEN COUNTENANCE

I have always been intrigued with the dialogue the Lord had with Cain just before Cain decided to murder his brother Abel. The Lord asked Cain a question that has stuck in my mind the moment I first read it.

> And the LORD said unto Cain, Why art thou wroth? and why is thy countenance fallen?
>
> —Genesis 4:6

An experienced and war-hardened Sergeant First Class approached me one day and informed me that he had a soldier that needed to see the chaplain. I scheduled a time to go to his unit's location on Sunday evening after I completed my worship services.

This soldier was one of my two Jewish soldiers and I could tell by looking at his appearance and body language that he was in big trouble. Immediately, this question the Lord asked Cain popped into my mind. I recognized him from four months earlier when I first arrived in Iraq. He had experienced some anger issues, and wanted to get them under control. We talked a bit, and as is my usual habit, I prayed for the Lord's Spirit and insight so I could understand what the young soldier needed from me.

He had told me that his father was a direct descendant of King David, so I began to think of how I could use the Old Testament as a tool to help him find peace. He had ambitions to finish his obligation in the United States Army, but then he wanted to move to Jerusalem and become part of the Israeli Army.

We shook hands, and as the soldier sat down, I asked him, "So tell me, bud, why is your countenance fallen?" This had a greater effect on him than I thought it would. He dropped his head and began to cry. During the tears, he mumbled that he was lost and didn't know how to get back on track.

I prayed with all of my might that I could feel the love the Lord had for him, and that I could be an effective instrument in helping this young distraught soldier find the peace he needed to survive the crisis he was quickly approaching.

We spoke well into the night, and I spent many hours struggling with the Spirit and the angry hate-filled heart of this young man with royal blood in his veins.

I felt impressed to talk about God's law, and had a scripture pop into my mind that I had never intentionally memorized. He had blamed just about everyone in his life for his misery, but he suddenly exclaimed, "Maybe it is God that I am so angry with. I could never follow a God that could allow my people to be murdered daily by Arabs bent on exterminating us."

I prayed again for further understanding and began to think about the great blindness of the minds and hearts of the Lamanites in the Book of Mormon. Sitting before me was a descendant of King David, with a good grasp of his own scripture, but he lacked the ability to recognize the application and practical use of the counsel found in the verses he obviously knew so well.

I marveled as I listened to myself question this young man, for the words and the direction of the questioning was not of my own design. I have done a lot of counseling, but never had I spoken with such a direct connection to the Spirit. It was not me talking. The thoughts and words were beyond my own understanding, but as I spoke them, they taught and edified me as well as the soldier that I was working with.

Toward the end of our discussion, I watched that young man weep heavily for several minutes. He had regretted saying that he was angry with God, and suddenly he felt the love of God in a way he never had before.

How grateful I was, and humbled that I could be used in such a marvelous way, to provide a fellow brother in arms with direct access to the Lord. Evidently this young man had a lifelong prayer answered during our conversation that night. In a small way, his life and mine were both changed forever as we shared our time together in Baghdad.

Before I left him, I noticed that his countenance had changed a bit, reviving and becoming brighter than it had been when we began our session. I mentioned this to him and he looked up. For the first time, he managed a genuine smile. I could see hope in his eyes, and I felt a tremendous gratitude to the Lord.

The Lord has provided us with the means whereby we can revive and restore our spirits from Adam's fall from the

Lord's presence. We have the tools of the Light of Christ, coupled with the Gift of the Holy Ghost to accomplish this task.

All that is needed is a desire to look beyond the parameters of our temporal and earthly vision, and attempt to see the world as the Lord sees it, along with the experience and feelings that will accompany it.

One way to do this is to go kneel down and approach the Lord in humble prayer and supplication, with the faith equal to the Brother of Jared, Nephi or Joseph Smith. The Lord appeared to these men and gave them direct answers to their prayers. This approach has not worked for me, however. So I have had to rely upon the insight and bits of light and knowledge that only come line upon line, precept upon precept (Isaiah 28:9-13; 2 Ne 28:30). I continue to study the scriptures and pray about the meaning and lessons the Lord wants me to glean from it.

It is our countenances that people will see first. If it shines, they will be impressed to look closer at us and learn from what they see and feel. I have learned firsthand that "Letting our light so shine before men that they may see our good works and glorify our Father which in heaven" (Matt. 5:16) is nothing less than the outward manifestation of our inner submission and obedience to the commandment to "receive the Holy Ghost."

With the Holy Ghost as a constant companion, people will see something truly different in our countenances. Hence Alma's question to those resistant brethren of the church:

> ...have ye spiritually been born of God? Have ye received His image in your countenances? Have ye experienced this mighty change in your hearts?
>
> —Alma 5:14

Those people obviously did not have the companionship of the Holy Ghost, and therefore had no light in them beyond that faint flicker of the Light of Christ, which most probably only burned bright enough to burn the conscience of each that stood to hear Alma's rebuke and invitation.

All things do point to Him, even when we fail to recognize the signs. The young soldiers I have worked with have given me important lessons on putting Christ first in my life. I have learned to recognize within myself the degree to which my own countenance reflects His image and light as I live with an eye single to His glory.

> *Behold, blessed, saith the Lord, are they who have come up unto this land with an eye single to my glory, according to my commandments.*
>
> *For those that live shall inherit the earth, and those that die shall rest from all their labors, and their works shall follow them; and they shall receive a crown in the mansions of my Father, which I have prepared for them.*
>
> *Yea, blessed are they whose feet stand upon the land of Zion, who have obeyed my gospel; for they shall receive for their reward the good things of the earth, and it shall bring forth in its strength.*
>
> *And they shall also be crowned with blessings from above, yea, and with commandments not a few, and with revelations in their time—they that are faithful and diligent before me.*
>
> *Wherefore, I give unto them a commandment, saying thus: Thou shalt love the Lord thy God with all thy heart, with all thy might, mind, and strength; and in the name of Jesus Christ thou shalt serve him.*
>
> —D & C 59:1-5

Perhaps one of our greatest challenges is to learn to as the Lord sees, to feel as He feels, and ultimately, to behave even as He behaves. Adam did fall that we could be, and I have learned that even in combat zones amidst death and destruction, life is joyous, and is a wonder to truly embrace and behold.

Learning to see life differently and to embrace what we normally would shun or turn away from is our challenge. I have been humbled many times as I have watched American soldiers find joy in service even during moments of great and intense life threatening challenge and hardship.

Adam did fall, and we are fallen, but do we have joy? I am often bewildered at how difficult we seem bent on making things. I have watched good American soldiers struggle with the most heart-wrenching problems. Despite their struggles and plights, they each still have duties to perform, and posts to guard and defend. Some of the greatest character traits our country has to offer can be daily seen in the comings and goings of our dear soldiers as they each struggle to carve out their niche and find happiness amidst the fray in which they have been thrown. And they do find it when they are true and faithful to their obligations.

Stonewall Jackson once gathered his officers early one morning during the Shenandoah Campaign. The Union forces were encircling his Brigade, and attempting to catch Stonewall by surprise. After prayer and deep thought, Stonewall decided on the plan, and then instructed his officers. His plan was to strike hard and fast at the Union's apparent stronghold directly in front of them. To the man, his officers thought him to be crazy and suicidal. Climbing up in his saddle atop his little sorrel, he adjusted his hat, looked down at his leaders, and said, "Gentlemen, perhaps we should not insist in this bold and courageous maneuver, but, it is our style, our way of life!" He was successful in breaching the Union's stronghold, and managed to push right through to continue to fight and make matters more difficult for the Union forces.

Adam did fall, and here we are! This is our style and our way of life. We must learn the laws that govern happiness and commit ourselves to them, then live them with full purpose of heart.

I have always loved the story in the Book of Mormon found in the eleventh chapter of Third Nephi. I have memorized this story in English, Japanese, and Russian. Imagery is a powerful tool that the Lord uses to touch our minds and hearts. I can vividly see the Lord descending from heaven and appearing before those ancient people on the American Continent. I can envision Him standing before them with outstretched arms and declaring:

> Behold, I am Jesus Christ, whom the prophets testified shall come into the world.
>
> —3 Nephi 11:10

After introducing himself, he then gave them very important information regarding peace. He said:

> ...and I have drunk out of that bitter cup which the Father hath given me...
>
> —3 Nephi 11:11

I have often pondered the meaning of the "bitter cup." What was it and why did the Lord use this particular choice of words to describe what He had done for us?

One morning I dropped off my eldest daughter at seminary and proceeded to travel north on the interstate to work. It was still dark, and I was on a stretch of road that didn't have street lights. It appeared I was the only car on the road that early in the morning. Then suddenly a car without its lights on turned onto the highway from the shoulder of the road. It pulled right in front of me. I was traveling 75 miles an hour and had no time to react. I went right through the rear end of that vehicle, spinning it off to my right. Meanwhile, I struggled to control my car, which careened to the left. By the time the dust began to settle and both vehicles were stopped, I was on the median still pointing north, and the other car was on the shoulder pointing south.

Everything had happened so blindingly fast that I didn't even notice the airbag deploy, nor did I notice the burns on my forearms from its deployment. I grabbed a flashlight and got out of my vehicle to go check on the occupants of the other car, a midsized Ford station wagon. There were several people standing around the car, dazed and seemingly looking for something. I peered into the vehicle and noticed two young men in the middle seat with their heads draped over the back of the seat.

My immediate thought was that their necks were broken. I had a sick feeling in my stomach, and began to pray. I noticed for the first time that I too was a bit dazed. I was fighting shock, but I was concerned about the two men still in the car. I reached in to check for signs of life. One began to moan and cough, so I felt a bit relieved, but the one nearest to me had no pulse.

I pulled him out of the car as gently as I could, and got him down to conduct CPR. But in the instant I was to begin, my mind went entirely blank. I couldn't think of anything. I remember growing angry, because I was well trained and experienced. I looked up, and around me were eight people. For the first time I realized that these were illegal aliens, all of whom had paid perhaps their entire savings to come to America and find a life of freedom and prosperity. I prayed hard for help, and suddenly a single thought entered my mind: "You have the Priesthood. Give him a blessing!"

Desperately I asked the people for this man's name, and all I got back were looks of confusion—none of them spoke English. Finally someone caught on and said, "Juan, he name Juan."

I put my hands upon Juan's head and quickly gave him a blessing. I was growing more desperate by the moment. I commanded that young man to live, at least long enough to receive proper medical treatment. And in that moment, my mind opened up, almost as though a portion of my brain had suddenly become unlocked, and I was able to conduct CPR. Within moments, he began to sputter to life. I was relieved, and felt that I needed to start mending the cuts and bruises of the rest of the group. I returned to my vehicle and retrieved my first aid kit, which is actually a combat lifesaver medical bag that has a bit more than just bandages in it.

As I returned to the other side of the road, however, my heart sunk. About fifty feet in front of their vehicle were two forms that looked like human bodies. I ran over to them and sure enough, two men lay tangled and broken in the dirt.

I got down and remember clearly saying to myself, "I gave one a blessing, I'll give two more a blessing," and in that instant, my mind completely went blank again. I remember growing very angry, and began to conduct CPR.

Going from one injured man to the other, I frantically worked on them for five more minutes. I could feel the broken bones and cartilage move freely in their chest cavities, and I was overcome with grief, and began to pray harder than I ever have in my life. "Oh Father, I cannot bear this burden! I have the blood of these two men on my hands, and I cannot bear it!"

Here we are enjoying a late-night feast on the ground. The temperature is about 110 degrees, and it is after 10:00 p.m. The camera's flash makes this setting look much different than it really was. We could not see what we were eating—and I think that was best.

My father sent me a couple of driving irons and a bunch of golf balls, so I would occasionally practice my swing and try to hit balls over the Tigress River.

This little girl was a delight, as are all the children in Iraq. I could spend an hour with the children and temporarily forget the war. Their eyes are filled with light and energy.

This is Sheik Fu'ad and his wife Noor. Fu'ad is sporting a bump on his forehead after confronting an Iraqi thief, "Ali-Baba" as we called them, and calling him to repentance. I think the thief postponed his repentance process.

I felt a heavy weight pressing me down into the dirt along the shoulder of the road. The weight grew heavier until it affected my vision and breathing. I literally felt as though I was being crushed and was doomed to die under that weight. I pumped up the intensity of my prayer and suddenly, almost as though I was snatched away from that early morning scene of death and carnage, I felt a presence beside me, and found myself looking down upon myself and the two dead men. The life-threatening weight was gone and for a moment, I felt relief. I watched as I continued to conduct CPR. I heard nothing, nor did I see anything beyond watching myself and the dead men, but I knew that presence and found myself drawn to it. It was peaceful and comforting. I suddenly sensed I was in a place far away, a place I have never visited physically, but that I have visited often spiritually and intellectually. I was in the Garden of Gethsemane, and I felt the presence of the Lord as He bore a much greater weight than I had that morning. I was humbled and realized that He had taken the weight off of me, allowing me to live.

Never in my life have I felt so separated from God, and yet at the same time so close. I marveled at how I could have peace in the midst of knowing the dead men I worked so desperately to revive had died because of me.

My mind never did open sufficiently to give those men a blessing, but it did open enough to thank the Lord for His great compassion and love He had allowed me to partake of that early morning.

I have spent a fair amount of time reviewing in my mind those events of that morning. I have analyzed and examined all of the possible lessons to be learned from the incident. I realized that I had knelt in the Garden of Gethsemane for a brief moment in time, and experienced a fraction of the agony and pain that was pressed out of the Son of the Living

God in that holy place on my behalf.

I cannot read or think of that event nearly two thousand years ago in a humble garden setting just outside of the walls of Jerusalem without recalling an early morning in New Mexico where I literally had the blood of two men covering me from head to foot.

I have gained a personal and intimate witness that the invitation given to all of us, to "come unto Him" will only lead to peace and happiness. There will be adversity and hardship along the way, but our focus should always be to remain centered on Him as we choose to live by His Spirit and to never depart from it.

Separation is not always an issue of physically leaving home or loved ones. Real separation, the kind that has the most devastating consequences, is the separation that occurs when we leave the presence of the Lord and venture out on our own, to kick against the pricks.

The Lord provided me with great peace even though I had the blood of two men on my hands. This experience has given me great joy as I have fallen back on it to help others cope with death and killing in combat.

Gethsemane means "oil press." Isn't it interesting that the Son of God entered into the Garden Press, and offered His life's blood to be pressed for all of us?

Olives are naturally bitter, but when the oil is pressed from them, the oil comes out almost sweet.

The Savior of all mankind allowed his very life's blood to be pressed from him as He knelt in that garden setting. And the sweetness of His oil for us is found in the peace that He promises us amidst our turmoil and hardship.

Christ did drink out of that bitter cup, and we really are on earth that we might have joy!

CHAPTER TWO

"CURSED IS THE GROUND FOR THY SAKE" (Genesis 3:17)

"For it must needs be, that there is an opposition in all things."
—2 Nephi 2:11

A soldier called and said he needed to speak to me. I didn't really know this young man well, but was familiar with his face from different unit functions. As we met, he began to ask various questions and shared bits of information that indicated he was hurting inside. I prayed that the Spirit would allow me to see this young soldier in the light of truth.

Suddenly, I stopped him amidst one of his comments, and told him that he was beating around the bush, that he had a serious issue and was not being honest and forthright. Stunned and a bit shocked, his mouth hung open and his eyes gave him away. I continued, "You are really here to talk about homosexuality."

His face instantly changed, and he grew silent. Tears welled in his eyes as he asked, "How did you know? Did someone tell you?"

I had to tell him that I had been praying that I could see him in the light of truth, and learn to love him as the Lord loves him. His tears fell, and after they ran their course, he asked what there was left for him. He was not happy, and blamed it on circumstances, wanting desperately to hear some words of encouragement that would help him justify his choices that had led him to where he was spiritually.

Homosexuality in the Army is illegal. The "Don't Ask, Don't Tell" policy is explained quite thoroughly, beginning at basic training and continuing on yearly through the units. This young soldier felt trapped. He was miserable inside, and struggled to find peace. He was raised in a Christian home with loving parents, and had attended church in his youth. Somewhere, however, he lost his way, and couldn't seem to navigate to the position he knew he needed to be. His parents didn't know, and he was afraid to tell them. He asked me, "What should I do?"

I prayed hard for wisdom, and for counsel from the Spirit that I might provide this young man with the direction he needed most at that time.

I instantly recognized a conflict within me. I had to put off a part of me that held an opinion, and search for and desperately cling to that perception that came from the Spirit that I knew the Lord held regarding the young soldier. I began to feel a peace and calm come over me, and suddenly, before me I beheld a different individual, for I saw him in the light of the Spirit, and not through my natural eyes.

I asked him how much longer he was going to dishonor his good parents by rejecting their good counsel and upbringing. Bewildered, he looked at me like he didn't understand, so I continued, "You have been taught one lifestyle, and yet have chosen another, one that is contrary to the one your parents chose, and through which you were created and brought into this life. You know the truth better than anyone else, and yet you mask and cover your choices with justification and deception. You cannot ever be happy until you let go of your desires and behaviors that continue to slap the face of your parents' teachings and wise counsel. The instant you stop resisting and rejecting them, you will begin to feel peace and comfort on the inside. You won't have to live a lie anymore, and you'll eventually be able to see the truth of how your choices have led you to this unhappy and destructive place."

Somehow this young man had gotten caught up in the briar patch of life, and had been torn up badly by it. Thorns and thistles were an understatement for this soldier. He woke up one morning and found himself in the midst of man-killing thorns that were threatening his very life. He was stuck in the middle of a quagmire where unwise choices had led him, and he desperately wanted out. He had a starting point, the one his parents had taught him, and he knew his current position. In his case, he needed to backtrack in order to circumvent the deep black hole of misery and despair he was in. It would take time, but he could do it if he could muster sufficient determination and inner resolve to walk the steady course needed to reach the destination his parents had raised him to seek after.

We are all going to experience sorrow, hardship, and difficulty. Not all of us, however, will experience the same degree of hurt and pain during our bouts with sorrow and hardship. Some will suffer greatly, while others will suffer mildly and minimally. I have always been fascinated by why this occurs. As a soldier of nearly two decades, I have long watched as soldiers of all walks of life have danced in and around sorrow and hardship.

Carroll Hofeling Morris asked a compelling question in the title of her book, "*If the Gospel is True, Why Do I Hurt So Much?*"

This is a question I have asked myself over the years, and looked for the answer in the lives and experiences of those I have served. I have learned that much of the pain and suffering we experience is due to the fact that we have not learned how to center our lives on Christ, and on His healing and saving promises. The ground is cursed, and it is cursed "for our sakes." This means that regardless of the trials life sends our way, our joy is to be found in the rubble of the wreckage, in the settling dust, or in the desperate moments when we think all is lost, where no hope seems to exist.

I imagine our first parents were overwhelmed emotionally when the reality of actually having to leave the Lord's presence hit them. Imagine how they must have been struck by the reality of having to exist and survive in an environment where thorns, thistles, and noxious weeds grew spontaneously rather than the fruit bearing plants of the Garden.

I have come to believe that the challenge that Adam and Eve were faced with was that of separation. Separation spiritually, physically, emotionally and intellectually.

Separation is also not always limited to physical location. Sometimes we become separated from our testimonies, or knowledge obtained by the promptings of the Holy Spirit. This kind of separation is perhaps the most subtle and most dangerous, as the widening gap between where we find ourselves and where we began greatly distorts our progress and affects our final destination. A testimony is much like having a spiritual Global Positioning System, (GPS) giving us a momentary position check, updating our position spiritually, giving us a clear mark of our position. This makes it easier to navigate further ahead toward our destination with greater accuracy. But as we become separated from the truth, from our testimonies, we have to rely upon our own intelligence, our experience, our dreams and imperfections. At best, we recognize that we alone cannot make it, at worst, we become blinded and hardened sufficiently enough to close out any further light and knowledge from the Lord to help us return to His presence.

For those who have not entered into the waters of baptism and received the Gift of the Holy Ghost, their inner compass is the Light of Christ, which urges and leads them to the truth. As they honor this light, it grows brighter and brighter and is often accompanied by brief flashes of the whispering of the Holy Spirit, confirming the truth they have stumbled upon. Those who are members of the LDS Church and have received the gift of the Holy Ghost must follow a different course. The rules of engagement are a bit different, requiring them to always walk with the Spirit, not merely enjoy brief flashes.

So here are our choices: walking with the Spirit and become essentially one with Christ, or to walk separately, and be separated from Christ. King Benjamin tells us that the "natural man" is an enemy to God. (Mosiah 3:19) Walking naturally, or without the Spirit, is to be an enemy to God. Putting off this natural man and yielding to the enticings of the Holy Spirit makes us saints and one with Christ, the opposite of being separated from Him.

Separation seems to be a common thread linking everyone in the Army to sorrow and hardship. I've noticed some common denominators, however, and have discovered that peace can exist amidst turmoil, hardship and suffering.

I have watched and marveled as soldiers in the heat of battle manage to find something to laugh at, or smile upon. Even with death, destruction, and danger all around, there is an inner need to be human, to reach out and connect with the life of another. When separated from loved ones, soldiers manage to make meaningful relationships and establish a sense of normalcy in an environment where all reason and common sense would dictate it couldn't exist.

Again, Adam's story in the Garden gives insight into dealing with separation. I can remember an experience while in Officer Candidate School, out on a maneuver. It was hot, and we were on the move, in the middle of a mock battle. In a moment of rest, while preparing our defensive position, I listened to a conversation between two Officer Candidates about the book of Genesis, and the story of the Garden of Eden. There was a bit of confusion and doubt about the story and the reason it was recorded. "What application was there in it for us today?" seemed to be the question asked by those engaged in the conversation. I asked a question or two and commented on my perspective of the scriptures in question.

Soon I was expounding all that I knew of the story, which came from my study of all the available scriptures. When I got to the part of the story where our first parents were cast out, the soldiers all seemed to chime in that it was Eve's fault—all of this misery we were having to endure belonged to her. I responded that I thought the most eloquent and powerful statement of honor given to a woman was given by Adam as he answered God's question, "Where art thou?"

I have found that this question is still in effect for us today: "Where are we really?" Are we standing inside of the Spirit's light, or out in the shadows of the lone and dreary world?

I have known the darkness of a zero illuminated night, swallowed up by the foliage and growth in the thickest of forests, not able to move easily for the vegetation, not able to see even my hand held directly in front of my face. I know the fear and uncertainty of being completely lost and off course.

Adam responded, boldly, and clearly, establishing WHERE he was:

The woman whom thou gavest to be with me, she gave me
of the tree, and I did eat.

—Genesis 3:12

I invited the Officer Candidates with me to pay particular attention to how Adam worded his statement, and how it is written. Almost as if he said, "You know, Lord, that woman you gave me and commanded to be with me, she was the one that had the foresight to partake of the fruit, and helped me to understand the importance of eating of it. Once I understood, I did eat."

I suggested that Adam was honoring his good wife Eve, and giving her the credit for enlightening him of the need to partake of the fruit, and then, he, Adam, alone made the decision to eat, taking full responsibility for the decision.

Somehow giving Eve credit took away the negative feelings those candidates had. One approached me later and humbly asked if I would tell him the story again so he could tell his wife, as he had never heard the story told quite like that before. It felt right, and somehow he felt good inside listening to and thinking about the events of the Garden of Eden. He told me that he never felt that Eve was to blame for our being here. He told me how he loved and cherished his mother and his wife and could not picture Eve in any less of a light. More importantly, he mentioned that it changed how he viewed life and the reason we are here on earth. Somehow taking the blame away from Eve gave new meaning and purpose for his existence. The master deceiver, Satan, wasted no time in deceiving the minds and hearts of men, leading them to believe that Eve was the one to blame for all of life's hardships and problems.

I learned a couple of important lessons that day. First was the power of a well-told story, with "well-told" not being nearly as important as a story based on truth and told with the aid of the Spirit. And secondly, perception is most usually our greatest obstacle. How we see things determines how we react or respond to them. This reaction will determine whether or not we experience joy and peace, or needless sorrow and anguish of soul.

Look at the next few verses as an example.

Genesis 3:14-19

> *And the LORD God said unto the woman, What is this that thou hast done? And the woman said, The serpent beguiled me, and I did eat.*

Eve, like her husband Adam gave credit where credit was due, but stood boldly and courageously, taking full responsibility for her choice and actions. Next, the Lord lovingly chastened them, telling them of the consequences that would follow their choices to partake.

Notice that the word "sorrow" is directed to both of our original parents. For Eve, her sorrow and the sorrow of all of her daughters would be found in child birth.

I have observed as a counselor that mothers generally take an exceptional position with their children. Mothers are more connected and in tune with their children, taking full responsibility for all of their successes and failures. When a child falls, it is mother that cries with the child. When a young man or woman falls morally, it is the mother that usually suffers emotionally and experiences great sorrow for the child.

> *Unto the woman he said, I will greatly multiply thy sorrow and thy conception; in sorrow thou shalt bring forth children; and thy desire shall be to thy husband, and he shall rule over thee.*

Eve was going to have to decide to separate herself from what she instinctively would want, and give her life for the lives of those she would bring into the world. A mother must literally change or alter her lifestyle in order to bear and deliver a child into this world.

The desire a woman must have for her husband is not limited to the physical desire, as most seem to interpret it. The Lord has woven into the fabric of women the power to bring out of a man the best attributes he possesses. Alone, man cannot achieve his greatest potential, but with the right woman, he can become as God is. The desire she must give also includes the desire to put him first in her life, to support him, sustain and comfort him. The woman has an inner sense of what is or will be required of her in her marriage relationship. Her duty is to respond to that inner sense and honor it. Like the child she brings into this world, she has an inner sense and desire to give to her husband the attention and care he so desperately needs to become great. So, along with God, a woman shares the role of the creator, creating life; not just the life of a newborn, but the life of her husband, helping him to change, grow and achieve the highest level of existence.

To Adam, sorrow was given by way of surviving and providing. The lot that has befallen most men is that of having to go out, often separated from family, and provide as best they can for those they love.

More arguments between couples at the end of a long day's work are centered over "who sorrowed the most that day." Husbands are notorious for thinking their sorrow is greater than that of their companion.

> And unto Adam he said, Because thou hast hearkened unto the voice of thy wife, and hast eaten of the tree, of which I commanded thee, saying, Thou shalt not eat of it: cursed is the ground for thy sake; in sorrow shalt thou eat of it all the days of thy life;

Thorns also and thistles shall it bring forth to thee; and thou shalt eat the herb of the field;

The pattern was set, and because Adam listened to his wife in the Garden, he would have ample opportunity to listen to her for the rest of his life, receiving from her spiritual insight and intuition.

The Bedouin women in the Middle East are known for their insight and the good judgment they provide for their husbands during trading deals, or visitations from outsiders. The women will position themselves behind a veil, a blanket or curtain of sorts, and while unseen to the visitor, listen and watch through a hole or crack. When the visitor is gone, they then provide their insights and perceptions to their husbands. A wise Bedouin husband will learn to value and treasure his good wife's opinion and input. She sees and recognizes things that he cannot, giving him valuable insight.

This kind of listening, however, demands valuing and honoring the things the woman has to say. Men struggle with this. Perhaps one of our greatest challenges is to learn to rely upon and trust the suggestions and counsel of our wives.

So, Adam was going to have opportunity aplenty because of the difficulty of the way. He would learn to listen to, honor and even value Eve's counsel.

The Lord lovingly chastens and teaches our first parents for a few moments by telling them that things are going to be different as a result of their choice. Where once they were able to freely partake of the fruit of the Garden—symbolic of the Love of God—they now would be cast out, and have to find nourishment in the herb of the field, amongst the thorns and thistles. It was not going to be easy.

Then out of love and compassion, the Lord instructs

Adam that in or through the sweat of his brow, he would eat bread.

> *In the sweat of thy face shalt thou eat bread, till thou return unto the ground; for out of it wast thou taken: for dust thou art, and unto dust shalt thou return.*

I explained to my friend that God so loves us that he provided a way for us to return to His presence. A way is provided for us to find happiness and joy here in this life, and in our joy, feel of His presence in the now. We can actually walk in His great presence now while in this life. I have observed that the sweat of our brow is the tears of repentance and humble submission to His will, recognizing that we cannot live happily without God's Spirit in our lives. I noted that the very first mention of bread appears in this story, and that it was synonymous with the fruit of the ground, and the fruit found in the Garden, which fruit was the Love of God. Now, suddenly, God was teaching Adam that a plan would be provided by which Adam could return to God's presence. The Bread of Life was being offered, even Jesus Christ, as Adam recognized his shortcomings, and approached a loving Father in Heaven with tears of sorrow and remorse for faults demonstrated or sins committed. The plan would require that Adam work diligently to overcome the flesh and the world. The task would be difficult and challenging, but the reward would be well worth it.

Sometime after our discussion, this candidate approached me and wanted to know more about my beliefs and how he could learn what I knew. I felt even back then, the Lord was working with me, molding me and helping me to understand a design and purpose He held for me at a later date. I just couldn't understand the whole plan at that moment, only that one was being put into effect, and that I was following it.

What I was learning was that a way was prepared for me to enjoy the fruit of the Garden of Eden, even the love of the Lord while being deployed to faraway places and being separated from my family. Separation from loved ones is in my estimation the most difficult thing I have had to endure. It is the cause of much depression and anguish of mind and soul. I have seen soldiers fearless in combat turn to alcohol, drugs and even attempt suicide as a result of the tremendous pain associated with separation.

Thorns also and thistles shall it bring forth to thee
—Genesis 3:18

During a four-year period of my childhood, my brother and I spent a great deal of time in the family garden. Be assured that we weren't there by our own choice. Before we could go and play, we had to spend much of the day in the garden pulling and picking weeds. My mother had a very creative mind and was able to provide my brother and I with ample opportunity to learn important lessons about life, while providing herself with time to read and study without worrying about the whereabouts and doings of two very active and busy boys.

The garden was BIG and always filled with plants of every kind. One cannot imagine the number of weeds that grow spontaneously and without invitation in a large garden, and when a young boy wants to play, work in the garden takes entirely too much time. Whenever my mother needed some time for herself, she would direct us to the garden and have us pull all of the weeds—not just the big and most obvious weeds—but all of them, including those seemingly millions of tiny weed sprouts just breaking the surface of the ground. There were at least twenty rows in our garden, and each row was perhaps one hundred feet in length.

Needless to say, my mother read a lot when I was young, while I developed a intimate appreciation for the statement of the Lord to Adam, "Cursed is the ground for thy sake..." Over the years, memories and lessons taught by the Spirit have served to provide me with an understanding that has enabled me to better understand the needs of others and to provide them with the help and comfort they need. I can testify that the ground is cursed, as I learned so long ago picking the tiny weeds out of the ground, one at a time, careful to get the roots to hopefully reduce the amount of time I had to spend in the garden the next time. I have relearned this lesson over the years as I have experienced a fair share of difficulty and hardship.

One of the duties of an Army chaplain is to provide counsel for the soldiers and their family members. I'll never forget my very first counseling session with a young soldier as a newly appointed Army chaplain. I was just out of school, had plenty of life experience under my belt—or so I thought—and knew that I had all that was needed to help this young soldier that was sitting in my office.

Within the first few moments however, I quickly realized that I was not prepared at all, let alone able to help. I was humbled and very frustrated at the same time.

It seemed I was in over my head. I lacked the ability to provide sufficient counsel or assistance to the soldier needing my help. I spent a lot of time in prayer and humble supplication to the Lord for help. I so desperately wanted to be an instrument of help and change for the soldiers I served. Somehow, I thought that in order to effectively be an instrument in the Lord's hands and provide effective and meaningful ministry, I had to be able to be a dynamic counselor. Over time, the Lord taught me and patiently worked with me, teaching me how to change my perception and align it with His purposes.

"Cursed is the ground for thy sake" has become a motto of mine. I have found peace in knowing and acting on the fact that the plants of any worth come only after the garden is sufficiently weeded and able to grow without the intrusion of the weeds that grow without effort. Weeds grow spontaneously and snuff out the potential of the good plants we painstakingly planted with the intent of partaking of the fruit.

I have learned that joy and happiness come only after I spend sufficient time daily pulling and extracting the weeds of the world from the garden of my heart and soul. Humble prayer and supplication combined with sufficient study of the words of the Lord and the instruction provided through Him to His prophets enables me to clear the weeds of my day, and enjoy the peace and joy the day really has to offer as I commit to serving the Him.

"IN THE SWEAT OF THY FACE SHALT THOU EAT BREAD…"

A young single mother came to see me as a last effort to avoid suicide. It was at the end of an already long day, and I was just closing things down and preparing to leave my office. My phone rang and on the other end was the voice of a woman who was obviously in desperate need of talking. She asked if she could come by, apologizing for the inconvenience and poor timing, but insisting that she really needed to talk.

She soon arrived, and as she sat on the sofa, she began to tell me all about the stresses at work, the problems of being a single mother, about the difficulties of being a female in the Army, and so on. Suddenly her eyes caught hold of a picture of the Savior I had hanging on the wall directly across from the sofa. She immediately broke into a flood of

This old gentleman is the leader of one of the larger Iraqi tribes, the Tamimi tribe. In his home, he has a carpet depicting the signing of The Declaration of Independence. When I told him that George Washington is my first cousin, eight generations removed, he got a bit teary-eyed and told me how he loved those men for what they did. He said, "No country in all of the world is as great as America, and these men made it that way."

This family lived in a modified rail car that had a dirt floor. They didn't have shoes and only the clothes they were wearing. Despite their obstacles, they were a kind and loving family.

These beautiful, innocent children who will hopefully have a better future without having to face the difficulties of living under Saddam Hussein's regime.

The oldest daughter in the family was nearly completely deaf. I arranged to get her some hearing aids, which improved her hearing considerably. I was also able to obtain more clothing for them from a family in the United States. This is the day her hearing aids arrived. She would grab my hand and cling to me with great desperation, so as to not let me leave.

An injured soldier is being transported to a safe location to receive medical attention. This was an all-too-common sight during my time in Iraq.

tears, uncontrollably weeping for several minutes. I prayed desperately for understanding and for a way to help this young woman, but as it turned out, I didn't need to say anything, as the Spirit of the Lord had whispered to her that Christ was her answer, and all she needed was to turn back to Him.

A young couple had been coming to my office trying to work out differences and get their marriage back on track. They had three beautiful little girls, ages 18 months, 2 years, and 4 years old. This was a mixed racial marriage, and it was the young wife that seemed most eager to fight to save the marriage, while the husband seemed less motivated to put forth any real effort. They were both sincere and honest, and they slowly began to apply the principles we discussed.

One particular day, they came into the office more frustrated and hopeless than I'd seen them in the past. We discussed faith, religious belief, and the importance of setting good examples for their young girls. Both the father and the mother sat up and protested that idea. Neither one had grown up with any religious instruction, so why should they need to raise their children in a way that neither one of them believed in? Silently I prayed for help. I struggled with how I viewed both the husband and the wife. I wanted to see them as Heavenly Father saw them, and understand his great compassion and love.

Suddenly a thought came to me to invite the two older girls to sit in my chair. Both came over, and even climbed up onto my lap, feeling important that they were participating with the discussion. I pointed to a picture on my wall of the Savior, and asked the oldest child who she thought that was. Without hesitation, she blurted out, "That's Jesus." Not to be left out, the two-year-old girl chimed in that the other pictures on the wall were also of Jesus, too. I looked over to the parents of these little angels, and both had tears streaming down their faces.

I asked, "How is it your two little girls know about Jesus, having had no instruction from either of you, and never having been to a church of any kind?" Neither one could answer that.

Many times since that family left my office, I have thought about the impact that experience had on me, not to mention on the parents. Where did their tears come from, and what was their purpose? The Spirit was definitely there that day. I felt it, and I know they had felt it. Out of the mouth of two little babes, parents had been brought to know, even if in a small degree, Jesus Christ. For that moment, they had partaken of a portion of the Bread of Life. They were filled with a sense of joy and peace the likes of which they had never before experienced.

In my own life, there have been many moments of silent tears, shed from an inner well of sorrow for things I had either done or had neglected to do, which separated me from the Spirit. I have also experienced shedding tears for those I have counseled, and the great burdens many of them carry.

King Benjamin in his great sermon to his people said:

> And now, I say unto you, my brethren, that after ye have known and have been taught all these things, if ye should transgress and go contrary to that which has been spoken, that ye do withdraw yourselves from the Spirit of the Lord, that it may have no place in you to guide you in wisdom's paths that ye may be blessed, prospered, and preserved."
>
> —Mosiah 2:36

How discomforting it is to realize that I alone am responsible if I walk without the Spirit of God. What jeopardy have I placed my soul in? While out in the wilderness alone, without the Spirit to guide and comfort, there is no "Bread" to eat, but rather, only consumable goods that come and go as readily as the passing of time, with the continual need to quench the pains of hunger and thirst.

I have greater respect for the events that transpired in that garden setting, where a loving and tender Heavenly Father prepared his son and daughter for the trials and challenges ahead. For listening to his wife, Adam was to be blessed, which blessing came by cursing the ground, so that it would always remind Adam to look to God. Temporal sustenance would come from the herbs of the field, but the life-giving "Bread" would only be available upon conditions of humility, repentance, and obedience. Once again, King Benjamin shed great insight onto this single most important of principles. He said:

> For the natural man is an enemy to God, and has been from the fall of Adam, and will be, forever and ever, unless he yields to the enticings of the Holy Spirit, and putteth off the natural man and becometh a saint through the atonement of Christ the Lord, and becometh as a child, submissive, meek, humble, patient, full of love, willing to submit to all things which the Lord seeth fit to inflict upon him, even as a child doth submit to his father.
> —Mosiah 3:19

I have often wondered if these were actually King Benjamin's words, or if he had gotten them from the Brass Plates. Were they written down from previous men of God? The entire discourse sounds like something Adam might have passed on to his children as he taught them to turn to Christ. Adam was cast out into the temporal world to do battle with the natural man. He understood from both divine instruction and personal experience that the only way to eat "Bread" was through the "sweat of one's face."

I can think of many instances where I have been so caught up in the temporal affairs of my life that I failed to look to God. A great example would be my assignment to Germany where I served as the battalion chaplain of a military intelligence unit. My family and I had tried to prepare for this move for more than six months. We wanted to minimize the amount of time we would be separated from each other.

Unfortunately, the housing office at my new location didn't want to cooperate at all. One week turned into a month, which threatened to turn into two. My focus was very temporal, and I could feel the Spirit leave every time the issue of housing came up.

The words of one of my favorite hymns came to mind, "I'll go where you want me to go, dear Lord." But then I would argue with myself, blaming the housing office for my anger, and for the needless separation from my family. I would say, "If they would be more organized and service oriented, this would all be settled." Two months turned into three which ultimately became five, and with each thought of the housing office and the people working in it, my blood would boil. I became very separated from the Spirit of the Lord.

My mind would clutter with such thoughts, filling my whole body with emotions of anger, frustration and blame. "But Chaplain Horton," I finally heard in my mind, "the Lord knew all about the housing situation here, and sent for you anyway. You have ample experience of serving in difficult situations, and have been given many talents with which to minister and most effectively serve His children in Germany. You have committed to serve him whether from a tent, a hotel, or a house—whether on the battle field or in garrison. He has only asked that you provide his good children here with your love for the Lord, your kindly spirit, and your desire to minister to their spiritual needs."

Once again, I was brought to remember my place, and responsibility. I discovered once again that I couldn't partake of the Bread of Life without one more time humbling myself and turning the matter over to the Lord.

Alma's counsel seemed pointed toward me and my situation at the time:

> Behold, he sendeth an invitation unto all men, for the arms of mercy are extended towards them, and he saith: Repent, and I will receive you.
>
> Yea, he saith: Come unto me and ye shall partake of the fruit of the tree of life; yea, ye shall eat and drink of the bread and the waters of life freely;
>
> —Alma 5:33-34

The fruit of the Garden was free to eat, and in abundance. Adam and Eve partook and were filled daily without any real effort on their part except that they had to reach for and take of the fruit. They enjoyed the presence of the Lord and basked in His light and love continually. But once they were cast out into the world, they were introduced to darkness and the bitterness of the herb of the field, not to mention the separation of His light and love.

We have been given bread to eat, but only after the sweat of our brow. As we humble ourselves and repent of our misdeeds, seeking His loving Spirit to be in us, we are able to partake of the Bread of Life, even of Jesus Christ. The real questions we need to ask are, "How hungry are we?" and "What portion of the bread do we really want to partake of?"

After my experiences in such places such as the thick forests in Louisiana, the Rocky Mountains, or the deserts of

Southwest Asia, I have learned that each journey demands navigation. My experience alone will not simply get me to the destination. I still have to have a point of origin, and must endure the hazards of the field, while trying to determine the safest and easiest way to my destination. Experience does, however, provide an element of peace amidst the trials of the journey, but each journey or navigation trial always carries with it a challenge and level of difficulty equal to my ability.

One of the dreaded responsibilities of a chaplain is to be present during the notification of the death of a loved one. In a deployed status, we receive notices from the Red Cross. The only way a soldier will ever be able to return home to be present at the funeral of a family member is to have first received the official Red Cross message.

Everybody deals with the death of a loved one differently. I have found that those with a strong spiritual foundation that are more connected to God seem to deal most favorably with death. Those who have less to stand on spiritually and intellectually, who are more separated from the Spirit of the Lord, suffer the most. Finding comfort during life's most difficult moments seems to be the constant struggle.

For the most part, I have wrapped my arms around many a soldier and simply shared the experience with them in a warm and tender embrace, then sometimes bearing my personal witness of a living God, and a plan whereby we may be together again with those that we love and have lost. I find that words don't need to be spoken nearly as much as genuine contact needs to be made. But when prompted, a Spirit-filled testimony is powerful.

One Sunday morning, while accompanying my battalion commander on a visit to one of our checkpoints, I received a phone call from my mother. My grandmother had died in the night. I love my grandmother with all of my heart.

I instantly remembered all of the times when I was much younger, getting on my knees and praying that God would protect and preserve my grandparents so that I could continue to enjoy them in my life. Finally, she had gone to the other side. I felt a tremendous relief and peace. Then, almost as an afterthought, I began to compare my reaction to my grandmother's death to the reaction I am so accustomed to seeing from my soldiers.

I realized that I felt no sorrow or pain. To the contrary, I was filled with peace and a sense of deep gratitude. Perhaps one of my best Sundays in Iraq was the day I received notice that my grandmother died. As it turned out, it was also a fast Sunday, which only added to the sweetness of my fast, and to the Spirit I felt all the day long. I felt a sense of gratitude that filled my whole soul. I felt truly blessed to be the grandson of such a grand old lady as my grandmother was to me.

Life is filled with separation, but separation does not mean that we have to suffer. Separation merely means we have the opportunity to count our blessings, and to bask in our gratitude and to turn to the Lord. Faithful "turning" to God brings us blessings of peace and comfort.

> *Come unto me all ye that labor and are heavy laden, and*
> *I will give you rest...*
> —Matthew 11:2 8-30

One morning while visiting one of our checkpoints, a new Iraqi female interpreter approached me. (Everyone seemed to approach me for something. Perhaps they thought I could wield some magic wand and perform miracles upon request.) She had a brother that was a major in the Iraqi National Guard, and he hadn't been seen since the war.

His last known place of duty was on one of the bridges that had been hit by our Air Force bombers. Her father and mother were worried sick about him.

This woman's father would walk around different neighborhoods all day, calling out his son's name as he looked for him. The family members eventually consigned themselves to accepting his death, but they needed to know where his body was to bring closure to the ordeal. She asked if I could possibly help find her brother.

I instinctively took the role of a counselor for a moment. I began to ask her questions, getting her to reveal her feelings regarding her brother. After speaking to her at length, I was very impressed by her inner strength and peace. She was saddened by the loss of her brother, whom she labeled as her favorite and best friend, but understood that God was in control and would bow down to His will.

I asked how her parents were handling the situation. She responded pretty much the same, however, as the father would spend his days walking the streets calling out his son's name, the mother would sit at home and worry, often crying about their tremendous loss.

My heart simply broke as I saw in this young lady the deep wounds of loss and separation from her beloved brother. I vowed I would do everything I could to help find her brother. She smiled and with deep gratitude thanked me. I uncovered several organizations that had records of both the dead and living of the Iraqi military after the war, but none of them had any information. I then turned to the Red Cross Civil Affairs department for a grave registration, but her brother was simply not to be found.

After an exhaustive search, I asked her how she felt and how her family was taking it. She smiled and told me that God knew where her brother was, and that her family would trust in Him to care for her brother. Now they would turn their thoughts and attention to living and continuing on as though he were not missing, because that is what he would want them to do.

I was humbled and grateful for having met this young lady. She taught me more about faith, trust and belief in a short couple of weeks than I had learned in a lifetime. Most importantly, she taught me how to grieve and experience sorrow without suffering. Her sense of truth was sufficient to enable her and her family to deal with the loss of her brother and find peace.

I can testify that the ground is cursed. I've traveled the globe and have not seen an area yet that is not cursed. I've witnessed great calamities, bloodshed and human strife. I've looked into the eyes of mothers desperately searching for meaning in the loss of a child. I've seen families without homes, food or any of the comforts that Americans take so much for granted.

I can also testify that in all that I have seen and experienced, the rest of the Lord's statement is true! "For our sakes" is the ground cursed. There is beauty, peace, and joy for the taking.

I love the comforting words the Lord spoke to Joseph Smith while he languished in Missouri's Liberty Jail:

> *If thou art called to pass through tribulation; if thou art in perils among false brethren; if thou art in perils among robbers; if thou art in perils by land or by sea;*

> *If thou art accused with all manner of false accusations; if thine enemies fall upon thee; if they tear thee from the society of thy father and mother and brethren and sisters; and if with a drawn sword thine enemies tear thee from the bosom of thy wife, and of thine offspring, and thine elder son, although but six years of age, shall cling to thy garments, and shall say, My father, my father, why can't you stay with us? O, my father, what are the men going*

to do with you? and if then he shall be thrust from thee by the sword, and thou be dragged to prison, and thine enemies prowl around thee like wolves for the blood of the lamb;

And if thou shouldst be cast into the pit, or into the hands of murderers, and the sentence of death passed upon thee; if thou be cast into the deep; if the billowing surge conspire against thee; if fierce winds become thine enemy; if the heavens gather blackness, and all the elements combine to hedge up the way; and above all, if the very jaws of hell shall gape open the mouth wide after thee, know thou, my son, that all these things shall give thee experience, and shall be for thy good.

The Son of Man hath descended below them all. Art thou greater than he?
—Doctrine and Covenants 122:5-8

What comforting words! What powerful insight the Lord has given us. I am humbled every time I begin to feel sorry for myself, thinking my lot is too hard, or the way is impossible.

All of my trials and difficult moments are for my good and will give me experience.

Everywhere I have been is the abundant possibility for happiness and the sweetness that life can offer, but for many, it can only be seen by changing the way they see it currently. The problem really isn't the problem. I've learned that by changing my perception, what I saw as a problem goes away, and I am faced with new possibilities and wonders.

THE STORMS OF LIFE

One Monday morning at the weekly Unit Ministry Team meeting for the brigade chaplains, as I took my place the brigade chaplain asked me in front of everyone if I was ready for the devotional. I had completely forgotten about it. During the week, I had managed to keep myself so busy, I never remembered that I had the assignment to deliver the devotional that Monday. Of course, being a former line officer, and never one to admit that I had dropped the ball, I replied, "But of course!"

My mind raced, and I prayed very hard for inspiration. It wasn't like I hadn't prepared and was asking the Lord to give me something for nothing. I had studied everyday that week, but I just hadn't focused my thoughts on any particular topic to deliver to several chaplains and their assistants, most of whom already questioned anything a Mormon chaplain had to say.

Everyone was watching, listening and waiting—and I was praying. Suddenly a thought began to develop in my mind and I posed this question. "How differently would the story have been if the Savior's disciples in that storm-tossed boat, nearly filled with water, had each simply resolved in silence to grab the ropes and rails of the boat? What if they had just hung on for the ride, leaving the Master to sleep in the hinder part of the boat?"

I have often thought about the circumstances in that fishing boat nearly 2,000 years ago, out on the waters of the Sea of Galilee. The storm was growing more threatening. The sea-hardened fishermen grew frightened and needed assurance—they needed comfort from the storm. All the comfort they needed was laying asleep in the hinder part of the boat, but they somehow missed that fact. They had all signed on to be His followers, and yet lacked the inner resolve and commitment to be true to their choice of who to follow.

I could tell by the look in each of the chaplain's eyes that I had captured their complete attention. The Spirit prompted me further. "Many times we turn to this story to give us comfort in the assurance that Christ will calm our storms in life, but notice how He rebuked them all for not having any faith for doing just that. Are we not also without faith when we wait to awaken the Savior amidst the violent storms in our lives, expecting Him to calm the elements beating against us?"

I grew up thinking that those hardened fishermen turned to Christ to save them, waking Him up from His sleep to calm the storm. I have come to believe, however, that I gave those early disciples of Christ too much credit. They had all the assurance they needed riding in the very same boat they were in, sleeping upon pillows. The storm obviously didn't bother the Master, so why should it have bothered those disciples?

I've learned that the Lord prepares us and teaches us sufficiently to accomplish our tasks in life. As I have studied and pondered that stormy night in the boat, I have discovered that the rebuke that the Lord gave His followers was to teach them to never forget that night.

In other words, Christ would always be there, resting in their boats, riding the stormy waters with them. All they had to do was simply look and be assured the storm would not eat them up. Their faith and efforts to build God's kingdom would not go unnoticed.

After the Savior's resurrection, each apostle of the Lord lived out the remainder of his life boldly proclaiming the gospel of Jesus Christ. When the social, political, and life-threatening storms arose, none of them wavered. They remembered the lesson of the storm-tossed boat and held on tightly to the figurative ropes and railing of their personal testimonies that they had received of Christ.

After my devotional, for the first time I received varying positive comments from each of the chaplains present.

The Spirit had touched them each in different ways. I was humbled, and again learned an important lesson. I too was guilty of waiting to turn to the Lord with fullness of heart until I had recognized myself in a bind. It is a lesson I want to always remember.

CHAPTER THREE

FOR THE NATURAL MAN IS AN ENEMY TO GOD

> *For the natural man is an enemy to God,*
> *and has been from the fall of Adam,*
> *and will be, forever and ever, unless he*
> *yields to the enticings of the Holy Spirit,*
> *and putteth off the natural man and*
> *becometh a saint through the atonement*
> *of Christ the Lord, and becometh as a*
> *child, submissive, meek, humble, patient,*
> *full of love, willing to submit to all things*
> *which the Lord seeth fit to inflict upon*
> *him, even as a child doth submit to his*
> *father.*
>
> —Mosiah 3:19

One day I had the impression I needed to visit one of my chaplain friends. I found my friend depressed, emotionally distraught, and filled with anger. He was burning out quickly. His unit had suffered more than its share of deaths in action. I told this chaplain that he needed to let the Lord carry his load. This statement only made him more angry, and he quickly countered with, "My heart is different than your heart." Now he was justifying his position of misery and discontent. All I could think of saying was that he was being a "natural man" and that in so being, he was refusing to let

God bring him much needed peace. My time was short with him that day, but I left by asking him to get on his knees and get confirmation from the Lord on "how the Lord wanted him to be. Abrasive and argumentative, and depressed? Or meek, humble, submissive, and able to serve?"

THE NATURAL MAN IS AN ENEMY TO GOD!

I have grown to love the above statement. It is simple yet bold. During my last deployment to Saudi Arabia in 1998, I felt compelled to read the first four chapters of Mosiah over and over. I would read them and think, "Now that I've read it, what now?"

But for six months, the Spirit continued to have me read and ponder the words of King Benjamin.

Perhaps I am a bit slower than most, but it finally dawned on me why the Lord wanted me to be so familiar with King Benjamin's counsel. All of my life I had categorized sin into two basic files. One category was for those sins that weren't very serious, and the other category for those that were. As a counselor, I see this deceptive ploy over and over. Somehow I hadn't quite made the connection on what the Lord has told us concerning sin, and His feelings about those little, supposedly "not very serious" sins in my life.

> For I the Lord cannot look upon sin with the least degree of allowance;
>
> —Doctrine and Covenants 1:31

We naturally don't like to admit to ourselves that we have chosen incorrectly, or that we are responsible for separating ourselves from the Spirit of the Lord.

A thought struck me one day while I was listening to a soldier unload his life's troubles in my lap. We were standing at one of our checkpoints protecting our inner "green zone" where we lived and operated. Iraqis were coming and going, and vehicles were being examined for explosives. Stress and tension had built to high levels within this solder, and his only coping mechanism left available was to spill everything. So, I listened, and this thought came to me:

"Complacency is the result of separating ourselves from the Light of Christ or the Holy Ghost. The Spirit will compel us to continually grow and progress toward becoming more God-like. In doing so, we become more faithful and worthy of the covenant we entered into at baptism to take upon ourselves the name of Jesus Christ and to serve Him till the end. We cannot become complacent when walking with the companionship of the Spirit. But in the moment we do separate ourselves from the Spirit of God, we begin to establish comfort zones, and in this we sow the seeds of complacency."

Each of us has an inner sense of what is right. We only have two choices—to either honor that inner sense, or to betray it. When we honor that inner sense, we draw closer to the Lord and perfect our inner character. When we betray that inner sense, we suffer in mind, heart, and soul, as we separate ourselves from His light, peace and love.

> *And now, I say unto you, my brethren, that after ye have known and have been taught all these things, if ye should transgress and go contrary to that which has been spoken, that ye do withdraw yourselves from the Spirit of the Lord, that it may have no place in you to guide you in wisdom's paths that ye may be blessed, prospered, and preserved—*
>
> *I say unto you, that the man that doeth this, the same cometh out in open rebellion against God; therefore he listeth to obey the evil spirit, and becometh an enemy to*

Here is the local school bus driving through Baghdad.
Obviously, no seat belts—or seats—are required in Iraq.
It sure beats walking in the heat, I suppose.

Here's another little family that had no home or money, but they somehow ended up living in an abandoned water-pump building at the south end of the 14th of July Bridge. My assistant and I paid them a visit one evening. That visit turned into many as we helped them with building materials and money as they needed it.

We would often perform routine medical checks for the Iraqi people in our area, and it created feelings of goodwill when we were able to help them.

Here are some of the many wonderful Iraqi children that I was privileged to get to know. I couldn't begin to remember all of their names but they all remembered mine—"Chaplain Tony."

all righteousness; therefore, the Lord has no place in him,
for he dwelleth not in unholy temples.
—Mosiah 2:36-37

I will never forget the impact a single quote had on me when I was attending my Air Defense Officer Basic Course in Fort Bliss, Texas. I was reading a field manual covering leadership and stumbled upon this quote from the Prussian general Carl von Clausewitz. He said:

> *"During operations, decisions have usually to be made at once. There may be no time to review the situation or to think it through. If the mind is to emerge unscathed from this relentless struggle with the unforeseen, two qualities are indispensable; first, the inner glimmerings of that faint light that leads to truth, and second, the courage to follow that faint light where ever it may lead."*
> —Carl von Clausewitz, On War

I knew immediately I had to memorize and internalize this simple statement. I have grown to appreciate King Benjamin's sermon, and the simplicity of his message.

OUR INNER SENSE OF WHAT IS RIGHT OR WRONG

Each of us has an inner sense of what is right or wrong. We each know what is required of us at any given moment, and each moment demands a choice. We either honor our inner sense, or we betray it. How we decide determines the outcome for not only ourselves, but also affects those around us.

Prior to deploying to Saudi Arabia in 1998, I was giving a series of predeployment briefings to families to aid them during their temporary separation. On one occasion, two single officers attended my briefing, and they became angry at some of the information I was sharing with them.

I was talking about fidelity and faithfulness in a marriage and remaining true to the marriage vows whether together in the same room or separated by many miles and extreme challenges. In the Army, a very common saying among soldiers, more particularly married soldiers is, "What happens in Korea, Saudi Arabia, Germany or wherever, stays there!" This becomes an excuse to deviate from marriage vows and other moral obligations to family.

The young single officers felt I was being too old-fashioned and unrealistic in my approach. They felt as though their chaplain was no longer approachable because of his supposed archaic beliefs about marriage and family.

What really got them going was my comments to the husbands in the group about pornography and any other material that would take their minds and hearts away from their commitments and obligations. In short, I was basically telling them that anything that compromised their integrity would only bring about more hardship, guilt and sorrow.

The young single officers were incensed. During our third month of our deployment, however, one of those young officers came into my office in Riyadh, Saudi Arabia. His eyes and body language told me that he was hurting inside, and he desperately needed to talk with someone that would understand.

I asked him what had made him change his mind about coming to me for any counsel, since he had made it quite clear a few short months earlier that he couldn't waste his time talking with someone so out of date and old-fashioned.

As it turned out, this young man had been caught with pornography in Saudi Arabia, a direct violation to a General Order. Punishment was pending, but that was not the reason he had come by. It turned out that his fiancée had heard about his trouble, and as he shared his arrogant opinion with her about how old-fashioned the Army was for pursuing such a trivial issue, and how inconvenient it would be.

To his surprise, his fiancée told him, "If you cannot be faithful to me in your mind and heart, then how can you expect me to trust you will remain faithful to me with your body?" She told him the wedding was off, and ended all communication with him.

The young officer was devastated, but he couldn't seem to grasp the concept of what his attitude and choices had brought him—misery and discontent. He said, "Chaplain, help me! I would do anything to get her back!"

The blindness of his mind and heart prevented him from recognizing the damage his attitude and choices had on others, particularly his fiancée, not to mention to himself. Suddenly, she was doing something very wrong in terminating their engagement, but in his mind he was innocent and his thoughts were completely harmless. His opinion remained, "Why was it that everyone had to be so old-fashioned and out of date concerning morality?"

That particular day, in my reading of Mosiah, these words jumped off the page and stuck out like a spot light, being etched into my brain forever.

> But this much I can tell you, that if ye do not watch yourselves, and your thoughts, and your words, and your deeds, and observe the commandments of God, and continue in the faith of what ye have heard concerning the coming of our Lord, even unto the end of your lives, ye must perish. And now, O man, remember, and perish not.
>
> —Mosiah 4:30

Here in lies the key to understanding separation. King

Benjamin is teaching us that even our thoughts will separate us from the Spirit of the Lord and place us in a position of spiritual jeopardy, while at the same time obscuring us from the truth of the situation. Evil thoughts can blind our minds and hearts, causing us to continue living outside of His light and Truth. I love the statement the Lord made to Saul as he traveled on the road to Damascus:

> *...I am Jesus whom thou persecutest: it is hard for thee to kick against the pricks.*
>
> —Acts 9:5

I spent considerable time with this young officer, and in our discussions, we spoke of integrity, faithfulness, and loyalty, and all of the attributes that make up our character. It was difficult for him, but he began to open his spiritual eyes to the truth of his situation. He finally recognized that his problem was not that his fiancée was old-fashioned, but that he had violated spiritual laws that governed his relationship with her. I eventually saw in his eyes a sense of peace, which begin to fill and permeate his soul, but only after tears of remorse and sorrow fell from his face and a change of heart occurred.

Lehi's vision and understanding of the Lord's program was clear. What is amazing is that he spoke not only to his children, but to us as well. I grew up knowing this, but have spent much of my life figuring it out and trying to understand it. In Lehi's vision of the Tree of Life, he saw mists of darkness, a fountain of filthy water, the river flowing from it, and a large and spacious building filled with mocking and ridiculing people.

The way to the Tree of Life was not easy to travel, nor was it clearly defined except by the Rod of Iron, which did not deviate from the course, but rather *was* the course.

To this young officer in Saudi Arabia, all I could do was

cry with him, and suggest that in order to win his fiancée's trust back, he would first have to become trustworthy. This would mean that he would have to completely change how he was on the inside, and to learn to look away from pornography, rather than turn to any graphic or written material that would compromise his integrity and lead him away from what his heart was telling him was more important than life itself.

I have heard so many times from people engaged in pornography of any form that "It is harmless and cannot hurt anyone as long as I keep it to myself." I once had a professor in my counseling program who taught that fantasy and even role playing is completely harmless and even therapeutic in helping to reduce stress and cope with hardships. I have always wondered how it is that these people who defend this compromising behavior never connect the dots and see it is that same "harmless" activity or behavior that has destroyed their relationships.

How powerful and captivating this blindness and hardness of our hearts becomes when Satan secures his chains of misery and discontent around us. The very poison that is killing these people is the prized nectar they savor as they develop a taste for it and defend it.

One afternoon in July of 1995, in the northern training area of Fort Bliss, I entered into a Quonset hut that provided my Air Defense Battery with a makeshift office for my orderly room and supply clerk. I sat down at my desk and saw an Army publication covering all of the schools for the different officer branches in the Army. I was at the time an Air Defense Officer and had entertained thoughts of attending the Infantry Advance Course after my stint as a battery commander. I picked the book up and opened it with the intent of reading about the infantry school requirements. The book opened to the Chaplain school page. Instantly a surge of excitement went through me, along with goose bumps and chills. I knew I needed to read the requirements. Of course, I ignored that prompting and closed the book, discounting my initial impressions. I didn't feel I had sufficient education or experience.

One more time I opened the book, and again it opened to the Chaplain page. Again, I felt a strong presence enticing me to read the page. I once again ignored the enticings and thought to myself, "This is too much of a coincidence."

Closing the book again, a thought began to occupy my mind. I wondered where the book came from in the first place, and even asked my orderly sergeant if he knew of its origin. He did not, and naturally, I thought that perhaps I had put it there not knowing what it was.

I had a strong sense I needed to open the book again, so I complied. Again the book opened to the chaplain page, and this time I read it. The Spirit testified to me that the Lord wanted me to be a Chaplain, not an infantryman. I could not deny it. Immediately I tracked down the LDS Church's Military Relations Committee phone number, and on my satellite phone I spoke with Brother Ellsworth, one of the endorsing agents for the Church at the time.

Two weeks later, my wife and I sat in his Salt Lake City office in the Church Office Building. He asked repeatedly, "What are you going to do when you are told by your peers that you are not wanted?" or "What if they say you are not a Christian and cannot preach at their pulpit?"

THE STORM OF 100 PEOPLE

I was a battery commander, and I told Brother Ellsworth I wouldn't tolerate any such reaction by my peers or other chaplains. I explained that I had received a personal witness that the Lord wanted me to be a chaplain, and by golly, that was all I needed. Peers and other chaplains who felt I didn't belong would have to deal with that issue on their own.

Brother Ellsworth simply smiled at me with a kind fatherly look that said, "My, my, another Ammon. He'll learn soon enough."

Five years later while serving in Germany, an entire congregation of about 100 people got up and walked out on me when I got up to read a verse from the Bible. They left the chapel and mingled outside the door, protesting my presence. I thought of Brother Ellsworth and his questions. I was humbled, and I realized that serving the Lord was not about "my feelings" but rather recognizing the opportunity to serve and maximize my efforts for the Lord.

Of course, I have the Constitutional right to my beliefs and the right to defend them. I am humbled at the thought of the great price that was paid by those before me—those who were brave enough to walk where the Lord led them, and who endured greater hardship and persecution than I have. They paved the way for me to enjoy the Constitutional rights to my dear religion, and more importantly, to serve my God as a Chaplain in the United States Army.

Satan's plan of deception is so cleverly laid, and he is waiting for us to stumble upon it. His plan ensnares us and binds our hearts and minds so powerfully that our greatest struggles in life become those in which we desperately try to free ourselves from sin's grasp. This deceptive plan involves taking our attention away from "glory of God." (D & C 59:1) If Satan can get us to shift our attention for even a moment, in that moment we become wrapped up in another glory and lose sight of the Lord's glory. We most often waste great amounts of energy trying to justify separating ourselves from the Lord's Spirit. Before we know it, we are out there all alone, kicking against the pricks, wondering how we got there.

I was humiliated and infuriated that day when those people walked out on me. What added to my anger was that the leader of the protest called later in the afternoon and wanted to come to my house to talk—not to apologize for walking out, but to convince me that I needed to give into their wishes and discontinue serving at their chapel.

I prayed with all of my heart for the Lord's thoughts on the matter. I knew what mine were, but Brother Ellsworth's patient, smiling face was etched in my mind, and I could almost hear him offering me comfort as I finally got his point. But I wanted desperately to see the situation and those people from the Lord's vantage point. A peace and an assuring calm came over me as I spoke with the man.

I learned an important lesson during the ensuing months. Somehow, I had managed to honor that inner sense of what was right, and felt the immediate comfort and calm from the storm that was raging about me. I was free from hate, anger, and frustration. I was free to communicate my testimony and desire to be faithful to God, regardless of how difficult the people wanted to make things for me.

I had to ask myself whether I believed for my sake, or are my beliefs for the Lord? Was I a chaplain because I wanted to be one, or was I serving as a chaplain because the Lord had called me to the service?

I hold true to my claim that I am a chaplain because I know that this is where the Lord wants me at this time of my life. I know this to be true, and the Spirit has whispered this to me. Nevertheless, in response to Brother Ellsworth's question, "What would I do?" I contended that I could not allow such unfairness and prejudice to exist, at least not when directed at me.

I felt as though it was my duty to stand up and resist

opposition and to correct any infringement upon my Constitutional rights. After all, I have worn the uniform of a soldier of the United States Army for many years. All my life I have testified readily that I believed in and even followed the teachings of the Lord Jesus Christ, coupled with my passion for my rights and liberties to believe so. It never occurred to me that the opposition that Lehi spoke of was directly related to any service I render to my Father in Heaven.

I learned that by seeking the Spirit amidst the storm, I had peace, and witnessed the impact and changes of the hearts of the people as they realized I had not taken their protest personally. I continued to be faithful to God.

They watched me simply grab the ropes and railing of my boat, and silently resolve to ride the storm out and remain faithful to the call the Lord had extended to me. Most of those that walked out that day later returned and became my best defenders. Most importantly, they each hungered and feasted on the Spirit of the Lord I provided for them when I preached.

One day while reading the Book of Mormon, it occurred to me that Alma and the sons of Mosiah, as well as those that they picked to go and preach the gospel with them, each suffered bondage, hardships, persecutions, prejudice, hunger, humiliation, all in the service of the Lord. In fact, almost as if by requirement, this challenge and hardship is pointed out early on with each description of their service:

> *And now it came to pass that Alma began from this time forward to teach the people, and those who were with Alma at the time the angel appeared unto them, traveling round about through all the land, publishing to all the people the things which they had heard and seen, and preaching the word of God in much tribulation, being*

greatly persecuted by those who were unbelievers, being smitten by many of them.

—Mosiah 27:32

The emphasis placed on how Alma handled this opposition is our guide to dealing with such opposition in our lives and vocations today.

But notwithstanding all this, they did impart much consolation to the church, confirming their faith, and exhorting them with long-suffering and much travail to keep the commandments of God.

—Mosiah 27:33

Moroni goes into even greater detail on how the sons of Mosiah withstood the blows of those that opposed them. I have grown to love and appreciate each one of those men for their faithfulness in such a difficult task. Each was endowed with different personalities and talents. Refined and used as effective tools, they handled each situation differently, but they all walked humbly with the Spirit and became effective instruments in the hands of God to bring about much good. Today with e-mail or the phone I can immediately contact the Military Relations Department and get guidance and counsel, and even complain about the difficulties I encounter. Ammon, Aaron, Omner and Himni had no one to run to with their problems except the Lord.

Now these sons of Mosiah were with Alma at the time the angel first appeared unto him; therefore Alma did rejoice exceedingly to see his brethren; and what added more to his joy, they were still his brethren in the Lord; yea, and they had waxed strong in the knowledge of the truth; for they were men of a sound understanding and they had searched the scriptures diligently, that they might know the word of God. But this is not all; they had given themselves to much prayer, and fasting; therefore they

had the spirit of prophecy, and the spirit of revelation,
and when they taught, they taught with power and
authority of God.

—Alma 17:2-3

This is very similar to a mission statement in a five-paragraph operations order. (A five-paragraph operations order is the official document by which all operations are ordered and conducted, of which the mission statement is the most important. It answers *Who, What, When, Where* and *Why*. When it is issued, it is repeated twice for clarity and understanding.) Likewise, Moroni repeats his emphasis on how the sons of Mosiah went about the work of the Lord.

And it came to pass that they journeyed many days in
the wilderness, and they fasted much and prayed much
that the Lord would grant unto them a portion of his
Spirit to go with them, and abide with them, that they
might be an instrument in the hands of God to bring,
if it were possible, their brethren, the Lamanites, to the
knowledge of the truth, to the knowledge of the baseness
of the traditions of their fathers, which were not correct.

—Alma 17:9

I am grateful the Lord gave me a few years to shift and realign my commitment before He allowed the congregation to walk out on me. My response was much different, having seasoned a few years, than it would have been in the beginning. I was able to work with the people as a representative of the Lord rather than as a brooding soul, wounded by the very group I was called to minister to.

I'm one of the newer chaplains on the block, but I have learned that without the Spirit I cannot do this job! Whether it is sitting in my office counseling a soldier or out on maneuvers with the unit providing worship

services, without the Spirit, I am nothing but another
uniform taking up space. I've encountered opposition from
other chaplains. I've been told that I wasn't welcome to
participate in worship services with them. My wife has been
shunned and even excluded from various wives' groups on
post because of our religion. At first, this type of treatment
was painful and difficult to accept. As I have encountered
such treatment, however, my mind has been directed back
to the template that Moroni provided so long ago. In the
seventeenth chapter of Alma, Moroni lists the account of the
sons of Mosiah to include their persecutions, successes, and
experiences with the Spirit. In reading Moroni's account of
the sons of Mosiah, I began to notice that even among the
LDS Chaplains, regardless of branch of service, the template
applies to each of us.

Each of us have different talents and gifts the Lord has
given us, and we attempt to serve the Lord as best we can.
At times, the outside prejudices and persecution seems
too much to bear, and is seemingly intolerable, unfair, and
wrong. Some chaplains handle it with a grain of salt, others
become very disturbed by it and suffer spiritually and even
physically for it.

How inspired Moroni was to take the time to describe
the differences of at least a couple of the sons of Mosiah,
enough to help us learn to be more reliant upon the Lord.
Notice that Ammon, after being captured and taken before
King Lamoni, addresses the king as a humble servant, yet
with boldness in his voice and determination and confidence
in his posture to win the heart of the king. Ammon told
the king that he wanted to be his servant. Aaron, on the
other hand, did not get immediately bound and cast into
prison, but was mocked and ridiculed, then forced to leave
the area. It was Aaron's lot to run into a more hardened
people than Ammon did, as he "and a certain number of

his brethren that were with him were taken and cast into prison." (Alma 21:13) But even King Lamoni was known for killing prisoners as it pleased him.

> *And those who were cast into prison suffered many things, and they were delivered by the hand of Lamoni and Ammon, and they were fed and clothed.*
>
> *And they went forth again to declare the word, and thus they were delivered for the first time out of prison; and thus they had suffered.*
>
> *And they went forth whithersoever they were led by the Spirit of the Lord, preaching the word of God in every synagogue of the Amalekites, or in every assembly of the Lamanites where they could be admitted.*
>
> *And it came to pass that the Lord began to bless them, insomuch that they brought many to the knowledge of the truth; yea, they did convince many of their sins, and of the traditions of their fathers, which were not correct.*
>
> —Alma 21:14-17

Moroni points out the conditions and hardships Aaron and his fellows endured, while also illustrating Ammon's reaction when he found them in prison.

Read Ammon's initial reaction when he met his brethren.

> *And when Ammon did meet them he was exceedingly sorrowful, for behold they were naked, and their skins were worn exceedingly because of being bound with strong cords. And they also had suffered hunger, thirst, and all kinds of afflictions; nevertheless they were patient in all their sufferings.*
>
> —Alma 20:29

Immediately behind our battalion headquarters in Baghdad was the Tigress River. A small island had been formed over the years on which a small community existed. Among the residents of this community was a farming family that literally lived off the land. One of the sons of this family had become a prisoner of the former regime, and had not been heard of since the war. The family had no way of knowing whether their son was still alive.

We inquired with the Ministry of Justice and searched their prisoner database. Thankfully we found their son in prison and were able to secure his release. The family was literally beside themselves with joy and emotions. The women made their high-pitched trilling calls of joy and gratitude, while the men were simply overcome with emotion. They all shed tears of joy and wanted to repay us for what we had done for them.

The son was in poor health, having been tortured and beaten. He had to endure terrible hardships and treatment at the hand of his captors. I spoke with him at length about his ordeal, and I was profoundly touched by his inner peace and calm. He held no hatred or feelings of anger. In his mind, God had willed the ordeal, and he had endured it. His only hope was that he had endured it honorably so as to please his God.

This young man had been taken by force from his wife and child before the war had begun and subjected to unimaginable tortures and conditions, yet had managed to endure the ordeal with trust and faith in God that things would work out in accordance with the will of God.

He had taken hold of the figurative ropes and railing of his personal boat, and rode the storm out faithfully.

I have marveled many times as I have compared the lessons this young Iraqi man taught me to the issues many of my soldiers have laid at my feet.

Every issue deals with separation of one sort or another. Each in turn provides an opportunity to either become bitter, angry, heart-broken and depressed, or faithful, trusting, spiritually focused and closer to the Lord. We simply have to choose and then enjoy the results of our decision. I have wondered how it is some people can enjoy being miserable, and how others abhor it. While some enjoy peace and happiness, others literally shrink from it.

CHAPTER FOUR

HAVE YE SPIRITUALLY BEEN BORN OF GOD?

*And now behold, I ask of you, my breth-
ren of the church, have ye spiritually
been born of God?*

—Alma 5:14

Becoming spiritually reborn is as simple as learning to recognize the spirit of God in what we see.

I had a Jewish soldier named Specialist Swartz, who had grown bitter and angry at the Iraqis. In his mind all Iraqis were the same—Jew hating, Jew-killing Arabs, filled with nothing but hate and discontent. After a short while in Iraq, this soldier developed a desire to kill all the Iraqis he encountered. I requested that the command allow this soldier to accompany me for a couple of weeks. I took him to meet some of the Iraqi families I was helping.

Within a very short while, I could see the hardened outer shell of this bitter soldier soften, and finally disappear. He became completely encouraged and consumed with helping the people. Some of the families welcomed him into their homes with open arms, and I watched this man become an instrument of change. He commented to me one day that he could no longer see Iraqis in the same light. Something had changed inside of him, and although he couldn't figure out what that change was, he was different somehow.

Specialist Swartz visits with two little girls who didn't have a home except those blankets hanging on the fence. Millions of Iraqis were homeless before the war due to Saddam Hussein's treatment of them, and they have scraped and made the best shelters they could, given the materials they could gather together.

This dinner took place one Sunday night in the home of an Iraqi family. We were discussing religion, and how God loves them. I often felt I was back in the mission field.

Here I am having a little fun with a cheetah. He snatched my camera case and wouldn't let go. I thought a little diversion with the sunglasses would help . . . it didn't.

These are some children that lived at a Baghdad orphanage we visited. The woman was so devoted to the children, and the kids melted our hearts.

This family was doing the best they could to stick together and survive some tough times. I was always impressed by the inner strength of these people. Despite terrible trials, the light of love and friendship would shine in their eyes.

As I thought of the change in Specialist Swartz, I believe he was beginning to experience what Alma talked about when that prophet asked, "Have you spiritually been born of God?"

Nicodemus is a great example of what being born again is really about for Latter-day Saints.

In the case of Nicodemus, the Lord acknowledged that in order for Nicodemus to recognize Christ and His divinity, he had to experience a process of being born again.

> *There was a man of the Pharisees, named Nicodemus, a ruler of the Jews:*
>
> *The same came to Jesus by night, and said unto him, Rabbi, we know that thou art a teacher come from God: for no man can do these miracles that thou doest, except God be with him.*
>
> *Jesus answered and said unto him, Verily, verily, I say unto thee, Except a man be born again, he cannot see the kingdom of God.*
>
> *Nicodemus saith unto him, How can a man be born when he is old? can he enter the second time into his mother's womb, and be born?*
>
> *Jesus answered, Verily, verily, I say unto thee, Except a man be born of water and of the Spirit, he cannot enter into the kingdom of God.*
>
> *That which is born of the flesh is flesh; and that which is born of the Spirit is spirit.*
>
> *Marvel not that I said unto thee, Ye must be born again.*
> —John 3:2-7

Being spiritually born of God is a process with specific requirements. The principles that govern this process must be followed and applied, or becoming spiritually born of

God cannot fully occur. This fact hit me one morning sitting in the mess tent in Baghdad. Have you ever listened to someone use words that didn't fit them? Somehow the words they speak don't match their character or personality. Yet they use certain phrases in order to impress others.

I heard a fellow chaplain trying to use military jargon in order to sound as though he fit in the military command crowd. His words just sounded funny coming from him. It was as though he wanted to sound like a battle-hardened soldier, but he didn't quite match the part.

As I listened to this same chaplain give a devotional later that day, I was struck with the same impression about his spirituality as I had been about his military bearing. The words he spoke just didn't fit the person. I sensed his words created a hollow and vacant element about him.

The phrases "God is great!" "God is King!" and "God is Lord!" were thrown out with frequency and emphasis almost as though he wanted those listening to be impressed by his spirituality; but there was none.

Becoming spiritually born of God is a transforming event where we become different creatures. Our words and actions become congruent with our character and nature. Everything about us seems to echo the same things we are saying or communicating.

> And the Lord said unto me: Marvel not that all mankind, yea, men and women, all nations, kindreds, tongues and people, must be born again; yea, born of God, changed from their carnal and fallen state, to a state of righteousness, being redeemed of God, becoming his sons and daughters;
>
> And thus they become new creatures; and unless they do this, they can in nowise inherit the kingdom of God.
> —Mosiah 27:25-26

How desperately many of us cling to our old ways and perceptions. Many of us expend tremendous energy resisting and fighting to hold onto our comfortable ways. We grow comfortable with HOW we are, and don't want to make changes in our lives.

What the Lord is wanting us to do is to let go of being natural men and women and to venture out into the territory of being new creatures in Christ, venturing out into territory that is well outside of our established comfort zones. This venture forward demands that we learn to look at and see the world around us differently.

One of my greatest challenges is to motivate others, primarily soldiers and their families to change their perceptions, to let go of their old paradigms and accept and shift to newer and more demanding ways of being. I encourage them to shift from being closed to truth, or to others, to being open and empathetic and giving to others. This is sometimes our greatest challenge. I know it is mine.

SEEING WHO WE REALLY ARE

Someone once said that we don't initially see others as they really are, but rather we see them as we really are. If this is true, then a very good azimuth check on where we are spiritually is to watch others. By recognizing ourselves in how we see them, we can immediately know where we stand with or without the Spirit.

To be spiritually born of God is to have greater portions of the Spirit with us at any given time. The presence of the Spirit in our lives enables us to see others as the Lord sees them, getting past our own prejudice and pride.

The whole idea is for us to learn to live and walk by the Spirit until our faith grows brighter and brighter until that perfect day.

That which is of God is light; and he that receiveth light, and continueth in God, receiveth more light; and that light groweth brighter and brighter until the perfect day.

—Doctrine and Covenants 50:24

As we look at others, and learn to recognize in them our true potential, our heritage and the Spirit of the Lord, our whole experience changes.

Our greatest obstacle, however, is ourselves! Because of our own stubborn pride, blindness of mind and heart, many times we fail to recognize in others their need for us to love them and serve them.

And I now give unto you a commandment to beware concerning yourselves, to give diligent heed to the words of eternal life.

—Doctrine and Covenants 84:43

One day an LDS soldier came to my office at Fort Bliss, Texas, and wanted to talk. He was serious and solemn. I invited him in, and as he sat, he struggled to control his emotions. He started by telling me that he was grateful I was there. Immediately, inside, I began to gloat. I was thinking, "Tell me more!"

He continued, "Being the only member of the Church in my unit makes it difficult at times to live my religion. Sometimes it wears on me, and I think I fall so very short from where the Lord wants me to be. To have you here, and to see you out and about boosts my spirits and makes me stand a little taller."

By this time, I was really feeling good! Yeah buddy, keep building me up, keep talking good about me . . .

Then, suddenly he humbled me. "You know, Chaplain,

the other day during that awards formation, where you were walking in and out of the ranks, shaking hands and talking to soldiers . . . well, as you shook my hand and looked me in the eye and told me you loved me, it answered a prayer. I was hurting that day, and suddenly, here you came. As you walked away, one of the soldiers next to me leaned over and whispered, "Look at that chaplain. He looks like Jesus Christ walking through our ranks."

With tears streaming down this soldier's face, he bore his personal testimony to me of the great love he felt from the Lord, and how his humble prayer had been answered as I, as an instrument in the Lord's hands, walked and shook hands during a normal day in El Paso, Texas.

Tears also streamed down my face. I could not control them, because of the Spirit of God that this young soldier had brought into my office. How grateful I was for him, and for his love for the Lord. I was ashamed for my pride and arrogance, yet so very thankful that I could still feel of His presence and be taught an important lesson.

How arrogant and proud we are without spiritual influence! I also had a prayer answered that day, and knew I had to work harder on seeing others as the Lord sees them, and not as the natural man does.

The Lord's guidance to Joseph Smith is also very important in understanding what we must do differently in order to walk and live by the Spirit. In other words, "Beware concerning yourselves." (D&C 84:43)

One night in Baghdad, a young lieutenant recently returned to duty after enjoying a two-week break back home in the states with his family. The Division had started a "moral leave" program and were able to send a good number of soldiers home for two weeks throughout the latter part of our tour.

Before each soldier could board a plane to go home, they were mandated to see a chaplain and be briefed on suicide prevention and reunion, or re-integration with their families.

I remember this particular lieutenant sitting in my weekly briefing, and seeing the excitement in his eyes about being able to go home for a short time.

My briefings are centered around making correct choices, and recognizing the importance of becoming servants and meeting needs of family rather than expecting to be catered to and loved any particular way.

I encourage soldiers to recognize the needs of their family and then set out to meet those needs.

This lieutenant looked like a horse someone rode hard and then put away wet. He looked tired and unhappy, so I challenged him. He threw me off by asking a single question. "Is it easier to respect people you are around every day, or those that you only see once in a while?" I replied that time had nothing to do with it. Respect could only come if one or all in the relationship are respectable people.

To be spiritually born of God is to be awakened, and to experience a whole new way of seeing the world around you. It is important to integrate respect into your character to the point that you engender respect in others.

Time is not a factor, because it doesn't make any difference whether you are respectable each and every day to the same people you are with, or to those people you only see once in a long while.

How you are becomes the focus of attention for those that watch and have experiences with you. Integrating the attributes of God's character into your own character forces change within, and it is this change Alma spoke of when speaking to his ancient brethren.

WALKING BY THE SPIRIT IN IRAQ

It was late in the afternoon at the security checkpoint on the south end of the 14th of July Bridge in Baghdad. The temperature was a blistering 152 degrees, and the sergeant of the guard called the chaplain, saying a soldier really needed to talk. I arrived to find a sobbing soldier slouched over, his shoulders heaving up and down. Next to his head was the muzzle of his M16, conveniently leaning against the track vehicle he sat against, and due to the security conditions I knew a round was chambered. My immediate thought was this might be this soldier's last attempt to save himself. I sensed that if I hadn't arrived, he would likely have killed himself. He admitted that adultery was the behavior that had torn his life apart—a shredded mess from which he believed there was no hope of regaining peace and happiness.

I quickly discovered that we didn't have any resources in Iraq to assist a suicidal soldier. We talked for a couple of hours, and not able to make any progress, I ordered the soldier to spend the night next to my cot. I embraced him and told him that I loved him. More importantly, God loved him and wanted him to have peace and joy in his life. Somehow, the soldier wanted to believe me, but was so consumed by pain and inner turmoil that he simply couldn't understand how it could be accomplished.

Nearly five days later the soldier began to climb out of the deep emotional hole he dug for himself. A smile would appear on his face when I would come around. He began to change, because he felt I truly loved him. I watched this soldier grow slowly but surely—he began to transform before me. I spent time teaching him about making better choices, and working to correct the bad ones he had already made. In this effort, he would be able to regain control of his life and find greater peace.

I spent time bearing my personal witness of the Savior to him, which he grew to expect and rely upon. The soldier is Catholic, but he is convinced that God sent a Mormon to save him. I have often marveled at just how the Lord directs His servants, and works in the lives of His children wherever they are, and regardless of their present faith or religion.

This young soldier had allowed himself to become blinded to truth and the eternal governing principles of happiness. In violating them, he had looked for reasons to justify his choices, and others paid the price. What he was really blinded to was the fact that his thoughts were leading to desires which ultimately moved him to behave improperly. This behavior ultimately separated him from God, and he wasn't able to receive any help or peace from Him. No peace, no esteem, no comfort or even any hope of being comforted began to take its toll. He had decided to end his life on a bridge spanning the Tigress River, so far from his home and family and loved ones. He could not feel God's presence, His love or His peace in his life. Thankfully he now found such peace.

A Red Cross message had arrived, and a female soldier received the bad news that her cousin had been murdered in New Mexico. The soldier's whole family was torn by the tragedy. The soldier had to remain in Iraq while her family at home tried to mend and heal from such a blow. Separated, isolated and alone, this young lady struggled with depression and anxiety. She wanted to be with her family, but could not. She began to question her commitment to the Army and the cause for which she found herself stranded in Iraq, about as far away from home as possible.

Suddenly the excitement of deploying to Iraq wasn't very exciting anymore. She struggled with depression and anger. I spent my time with her sharing my witness of life after death, and the eternal plan for the family. Somehow she found comfort in our conversations, but still struggled greatly with her own separation issues. First, she was separated from home and family, but most importantly, she was separated from God and the teachings of her youth. She knew she needed to be more faithful and diligent in worshipping God.

A soldier's wife in Germany was diagnosed with cancer and needed to undergo chemotherapy. Because of the demands to make mission, the soldier was not allowed to return home after receiving a Red Cross message requesting his presence. His wife had three young kids, all very active and demanding attention. With his wife undergoing chemo, she would not be able to fully attend to the children. The soldier's mind was not on his work. He was miserable, and he constantly needed to see the chaplain for counseling and comfort.

A young female soldier approached me one evening and had a serious look in her eyes. She was obviously shaken a bit, so I asked her what was bothering her. She described a routine patrol mission she had participated in that day. Somehow, in the process of events, she found herself alone guarding the vehicles and sensitive items while everyone else were investigating something suspicious. Suddenly an Iraqi male approached her with what she described as an angry face and his hands behind his back. She was terrified, and she yelled for the man to stop. He ignored her shouts and continued toward her. Her weapon, a squad automatic weapon (SAW) was loaded and now pointing directly at the man. She yelled for him to stop once again, and when he refused, she took the weapon off "safety" and began to squeeze the trigger. She told me that her heart was pounding. Then for some reason, at that instant, something caught the man's attention to his side. He turned just enough so she could see his hands were empty. She relaxed her grip on the trigger, but remained shaken at how close she had come to killing a man.

The thought that she had nearly sent a man to his grave, separating him from this life, his family and friends, left her unsettled to say the least. She wondered about God's plan for life, and what role she played in it. In addition to being shaken from her experience, she sensed inside a separation of sorts from what she felt was right and important. As the Psalmist said:

> *My God, my God, why hast thou forsaken me? why art thou so far from helping me, and from the words of my roaring?*

> —Psalms 22:1

ADVERSITY AND OPPORTUNITY

I sat in the large palace that once belonged to Saddam Hussein, listening and speaking with an Iraqi gentleman I met a few weeks earlier. He was asking me questions about religion and expressing his personal feelings about the world situation and the hate that seems so abundant. He asked, "Why does America so readily listen to and help the Jewish people over the Arab people?"

With each of his questions, I would always reply with a brief testimony of God, and the importance to live a life centered on God. Finally, out of exasperation, he exclaimed, "You always are so positive and happy. Do you have problems like normal people?" At first, I wasn't sure I had heard him right, so I asked him to repeat his question. He reworded it the second time and asked, "You don't seem to have troubles in your life like normal men. Do you have problems in your life?"

I smiled and assured him I was every bit as normal as he was, but I had learned to look at life's challenges as opportunities for growth and to demonstrate my love for God.

A broad smile grew on his face, and he said, "So, you have opportunities where I have problems. I love my God, so why do I have problems and you don't?"

I was reminded of a statement in a movie I had recently seen where a probing question was asked, and the answer was summed up in five words, "That's right, perception is everything!" Sitting across from this Iraqi man I had learned a facet of a truth I had always known, but hadn't really truly understood until it suddenly became clear to me.

Adversity is a constant element of life. We are told in the scriptures that there must needs be an opposition in all things. (2 Ne 2:11) With adversity comes the reality of hardship, which, depending on our perception, will determine our state of mind, and state of being.

King Benjamin instructs us that the natural man is an enemy to God and has been from the fall of Adam and will be forever and ever... (Mosiah 3:19)

Our state of mind and state of being is what makes us enemies or saints, according to King Benjamin. Whether we are enemies to God or saints is completely a function of how we are, rather than what we do. Nephi spoke of the "blindness of their minds" being the cause of being brought down into captivity. (1 Ne 14:7) Jarom said that much should be done among his people because of the hardness of their hearts, the deafness of their ears and the blindness of their minds. (Jarom 1:3) King Benjamin's guidance on becoming a saint is very simple, but requires completely changing the way we see and think, ultimately changing the way we feel and then behave. In order to put off the natural man, we must learn to yield to the enticings of the Holy Spirit, and become a saint through the atonement of Christ the Lord. We must become as a child, submissive, meek, humble, patient, full of love, and willing to submit unto all things the father seeth fit to inflict upon us, "even as a child doth submit unto his father." (Mosiah 3:19)

I know an Imam—a Muslim cleric—named Fuaad, a delightful man whom I have grown very fond of. Unfortunately, he was mistreated by an American soldier at a checkpoint. The soldier was manning a post in 135 degree weather and was most likely feeling a bit overwhelmed by the large number of Iraqis crowding him. Perhaps he even felt a bit threatened by their insistence on being heard. As my friend approached the soldier, trying to provide an explanation in his broken English, the soldier became hostile, yelling at the cleric to shut up and get back.

When the cleric continued to press, he found himself at gun point, cuffed, dragged off to the side and frisked from head to foot. For this Imam, such treatment in front of all of those people was clearly a violation bordering on rape. He viewed himself as a holy man, a priest not to be touched by the hands of an unclean man.

A day after it happened, I visited Fuaad and found him in bed, crying and suffering greatly. He had lost his dignity, and his presence in front of the people as a priest. He was no longer regarded as untouchable and pure. In his broken English he kept repeating to me, "I am no longer a priest! I have been shamed in front of my people."

It was obvious that this man had suffered considerable emotional damage, not to mention the damage to his credibility and reputation. He was devastated, and as I looked at him laying in his bed, crying and not able to look up into my eyes, I took his hand and asked, "What does your love for God and for all men demand you do?"

This came as a completely foreign concept to him. His look was more like a deer in the headlights. "What do you mean my love of God? How could God allow such a thing to happen to me? I have served him faithfully with all my heart, and yet He has abandoned me."

I suddenly felt something I couldn't quite explain, yet knew it was familiar. Later as I read in First Nephi, suddenly it all came into perspective to me.

> But it came to pass that I prayed unto the Lord, saying: O Lord, according to my faith which is in thee, wilt thou deliver me from the hands of my brethren; yea, even give me strength that I may burst these bands with which I am bound.
>
> —1 Nephi 7:17

I had grown to love this Muslim priest, and had shared much with him regarding religion and my testimony. I even gave him a copy of the Book of Mormon in Arabic, which he treated as though is were really a prized possession by kissing it and holding it to his forehead. And yet, suddenly faced with a hardship—a challenge of mind and heart—he had no means with which to cope with it. He had lived his entire life dedicated to God and teaching the people to love God and devote their lives to Him, yet when his own state of mind and way of being with God had been challenged, and he found himself short.

I realized that "doing" for God was not nearly enough. I have learned that before I *do* anything for the Lord, I first must *be* right before the Lord. Another verse came to my mind:

But behold, I say unto you that ye must pray always, and not faint; that ye must not perform any thing unto the Lord save in the first place ye shall pray unto the Father in the name of Christ, that he will consecrate thy performance unto thee, that thy performance may be for the welfare of thy soul.

—2 Nephi 32:9

I wonder how often we find ourselves in a similar situation. On the one hand, we claim to believe, and thus live our lives until we are faced with a seemingly insurmountable challenge which taxes our relationship with God, and how we perceive our relationship with Him.

When the dust of hardship settles, we find ourselves either as enemies of God, or as saints. We either honor our sense of what is right and what we should do in response to the hardships we face, or we cave in and betray that inner sense and react completely contrary to what our testimonies and the enticings of the Holy Spirit—or the Light of Christ which is in all of us—demand that we do.

It has been said that adversity proves whom God can trust. This is true in looking at the bigger picture, but at the smaller and inner picture of the heart and mind, adversity is the sand paper that smooths our rough surface of unbelief, the light of understanding that chases the darkness away. That is only true if we approach adversity and hardship in the appropriate way. If not, adversity will only serve to harden an already hardened heart, and continue to bind and blind our minds and our hearts so that we can't clearly see the truth of the situation.

In reality, life is nothing more than a proving ground, where we are tested and tried. The adversity of life proves which of God's children are truly trustworthy and can be counted on to do the right thing.

The Lord's gentle reminder to Joseph Smith that he was "not yet like unto Job" comforts me. As I have read and pondered the Prophet Joseph's story, I have marveled at just how difficult it was for him. Yet he managed to honorably get through the hardship and adversity. To know that there was a mortal man that endured even greater hardships and adversity—and made it through—adds comfort and lends hope that I too can endure it.

Elaine Cannon in her book, *Adversity,* wrote:

> *Adversity proves whom God can trust. Who of us, as Job did, will stand firm, be obedient, and love God no matter what comes into our lives? We are proven through adversity.*
>
> *Whom can God trust? Who will suffer appropriately in order to learn the lessons, be the example of a believer and a witness to the hand of God in the affairs of man? Who will endure trials to help in the work of the kingdom of God on earth?* (Elaine Cannon, *Adversity,* Bookcraft, 1987, p. 32.)

Sister Cannon asks, "Who will suffer appropriately in order to learn the lessons?" The word "appropriately" being the key to learning how to confront and work through difficulty and hardship.

We are all going to have to face adversity, hardship and sorrow, but, none of us really have to suffer! Suffering appropriately is another way of saying, "Sorrow appropriately" or "Experience hardship appropriately."

The appropriate way in which to experience hardship is to do it with an eye single to the glory of God. We must recognize that adversity is part of the Lord's program for our growth and development. This approach to experiencing hardship changes all of the rules, and provides us with different solutions to our trials. We do have to experience sorrow, but we don't have to suffer in our sorrow.

> *Be thou humble; and the Lord thy God shall lead thee by the hand, and give thee answer to thy prayers.*
>
> *I know thy heart, and have heard thy prayers concerning thy brethren. Be not partial towards them in love above many others, but let thy love be for them as for thyself; and let thy love abound unto all men, and unto all who love my name.*
>
> *And pray for thy brethren of the Twelve. Admonish them sharply for my name's sake, and let them be admonished for all their sins, and be ye faithful before me unto my name.*
>
> *And after their temptations, and much tribulation, behold, I, the Lord, will feel after them, and if they harden not their hearts, and stiffen not their necks against me, they shall be converted, and I will heal them.*
>
> *Now, I say unto you, and what I say unto you, I say unto all the Twelve: Arise and gird up your loins, take up your cross, follow me, and feed my sheep.*
>
> —Doctrine and Covenants 112:10-14

One of the many things that chaplains do for their units is to provide briefings covering various topics. Shortly after arriving in Iraq, I began conducting briefings for each of the companies covering suicide prevention, principle-centered living, and reunion preparation.

My experience has been that soldiers will tell you by their body language and facial expressions whether they agree with what you are telling them. My first time doing these briefings came before a hardened crowd—soldiers in a combat zone that had survived hardships and danger before

One of the many palaces Saddam Hussein built for his family and inner circle, while millions of his people went hungry.

The unending heat made perspiration a constant part of life for everyone, particularly the soldiers.

We met this farmer and his sons on the back side of Janain, the small island right behind the palace I lived in. I admired them for making the best of their humble circumstances.

A happy reunion with Chaplain Raeolina. This chaplain has a heart of gold. I love him a lot, and so do his soldiers! He had been in Iraq for two months before I got there. It was good to see him.

I arrived. Who did I think I was, and what was I going to tell them that they hadn't already figured out?

I took a vastly different approach to the suicide prevention brief. I taught gospel principles, how to make correct choices, and how to avoid consequences that cause stress and rip apart relationships.

I had their undivided attention! Some of the soldiers were squirming in their seats as they listened.

Many soldiers approached me and commented on how the briefing I had given was the best they'd had in the Army. Many soldiers approached me and revealed things that they never would have told me prior to the briefing. One soldier, with tears in his eyes, said that as he thought about what I said, he realized that he was one of the people at risk, and that thought had humbled him.

He had made some bad choices, and had paid a heavy price emotionally as well as in his marriage. It was liberating for him to realize that his stress and bouts with depression were a result of poor choices he had made.

We talked about changing his thoughts, and then ultimately his desires and behaviors. This idea further liberated this young soldier and made him optimistic for the first time in a long time. His disposition had changed in moments, and I could see that he was beginning to change from within.

> But this much I can tell you, that if ye do not watch yourselves, and your thoughts, and your words, and your deeds, and observe the commandments of God, and continue in the faith of what ye have heard concerning the coming of our Lord, even unto the end of your lives, ye must perish. And now, O man, remember, and perish not.
>
> —Mosiah 4:30

Some of the greatest challenges I have encountered have been those challenges that occurred in the recesses of my mind. I seek to be spiritually ready to accept the whisperings of the Holy Ghost and to be able to readily accept spiritual guidance on what to do, where to go, and how to approach a certain task or person. I have learned that my thoughts are powerful and impact my life and those around me. When my thoughts betray or offend the Spirit, then my demeanor diminishes somehow. I change inside slightly, but sufficiently to affect others around me.

Have you ever experienced seeing someone you care for and knowing that something is not quite right with them? You may have asked, "What is wrong?" Did your question and concern come from anything they said, or from what you felt or perceived in their presence?

Conversely, being spiritually born of God is an event that changes an individual sufficiently that others will readily recognize something different in their countenance, their demeanor, and their overall attitude.

The change is powerful and moves us to further grow and develop spiritually.

TAKING THE HORSE TO THE WATER AND MAKING IT DRINK

It is generally accepted the you cannot take a horse to water and make it drink. This saying is used to remind people that it is fruitless to try to change another person. People are going to do and be who they want to be. Much of my counseling in Baghdad consisted of marriage issues. I often heard questions like "How can I change her mind?" or "What can I do to make her love me more?" My favorite was, "If only I could be home, I could fix things and make them better!"

One soldier approached me two days after Christmas. He looked tired and emotionally drained. I could tell he didn't have a good Christmas and hungered spiritually. As he began to speak, emotions that had been pent up inside began to work their way out through tears and he showed embarrassment for such an outward display.

His wife was struggling with depression and had decided to see a doctor for her condition. The soldier said that he felt like a failure and needed to "be there for his wife." I asked him what "being there" meant. His response was to give her support and love.

I allowed his emotions to run their course, and then I asked him if he ever experienced a moment when sitting right next to his dear wife, the he ever felt alone or disconnected from her. Immediately he replied, "Many times."

I then again asked this young soldier what "being there" really meant. Obviously "being there" with her geographically and physically didn't fulfill or satisfy his inner need to connect with her. How was being there now going to change anything?

A light began to flicker in his eyes, and I could tell he was beginning to get a glimpse of what I meant. As we discussed the matter more deeply, this young soldier began to realize that he was virtually helpless to make his wife think or feel anything, but that he could at least influence her thoughts and feelings by changing the way he treats her.

A natural man approach to any of the issues dealing with marriage separation is to look for reasons *why* the horse is not drinking from the water trough provided.

Knowing the horse will not be forced to drink, we continually look for a way to coerce or deceive the horse into drinking. Or perhaps we even create a greater thirst within the horse by working it harder. But in the final analysis, I have not ever seen it work.

Being born of the Spirit of the Lord, however, provides a way to inspire the horse to drink on its own from the waters provided. If we could always remember that the Lord Himself uses the illustration of "drinking from the waters of life," we would better understand how to inspire and motivate others to drink as well.

> *Behold, he sendeth an invitation unto all men, for the arms of mercy are extended towards them, and he saith: Repent, and I will receive you.*
>
> *Yea, he saith: Come unto me and ye shall partake of the fruit of the tree of life; yea, ye shall eat and drink of the bread and the waters of life freely;*
>
> —Alma 5:33-34

I'll relate an experience I had when I was twelve years old. I spent the summer with my grandfather, one of the last true cowboys in the West. He and my uncle ran over 6,000 head of cattle a year in southern California. Living and working in the Imperial Valley, he would move his cattle from one freshly harvested field to another, with the crops varying from sugar beats to carrots.

Each bunch of cattle consisted of up to 400 head. Sometimes a cattle drive would be ten miles long, taking several hours. Because of the high heat in the summer, much of a move would take place in the early morning hours to conserve the fat on the cattle.

I had a mare I dearly loved named Juanita. She had saved my life on several occasions, and I felt a tender affection toward her. Always concerned about her, I wanted to be sure she had plenty of water at the end of our drives, but she would never drink. I'd get angry at her, even fighting her to get her to drink. She never would drink.

One day my grandfather watched me fighting my horse to drink, then he rode up to the very trough I was at, got down and loosened his saddle. Rubbing his horse down a bit, he took the bridle off and dropped it to the ground, then stepped back.

His horse slowly walked up to the trough and drank his fill. Then the horse backed off and stood waiting for my grandfather to re-bridle and tighten the saddle. After getting back in his saddle and turning to ride off, my wise grandfather simply stopped and said, "Don't be at it all day, son. We still have work to do."

My grandfather had managed to teach me perhaps the most important lesson I have ever learned, and he did it without saying anything. It was *how* he was that caught my attention and taught me the lesson.

I learned that you *can* take a horse to water and make him drink. The trick is, the horse has to sense sincerity and genuineness—and know that the choice is his. Then he will drink. Joseph Smith was asked how he managed to lead such an industrious and hard-working people. He replied, "I teach them correct principles, and they govern themselves." (*Collected Discourses,* 1886-1898, Vol 3.)

Imitating my grandfather's example, I did as he had done with his horse, and watched in amazement and awe. My horse walked up to the trough and drank.

I had changed significantly by watching my grandfather. His example had taught me to put the needs of my horse ahead of my own needs. I have found that the more like the Savior I strive to become, the more I am compelled to put the needs of others ahead of my own needs, and the more genuine I become. I truly desire to become a blessing to those around me.

Being Spiritually Born of God is a mighty change that

takes place within the hearts of men, changing them to the degree they are spiritually centered.

Just behind the New Presidential Palace that I lived in along the Tigress River, there is a small island called Janain, on which resides a community of more than twenty families. This small area was within my unit's area of responsibility, therefore, I made it a point to spend some of my time among those families. I loved to spend time with the children. They somehow made being in a combat zone more enjoyable. There is always a sense of ease and an air of fun when children are around. Innocence is the same regardless of where you are, and during Operation Iraqi Freedom, being around the children of Janain brought me great joy and peace.

Among this group was the Kassup family, who stood out from the very first time I saw them. The children were somehow different from all of the other kids. The parents radiated a different light than the other adults. Inside of their home was a sweet spirit of love and peace.

I was always taking pictures of the people with my digital camera, and one day I managed to find a color printer. I printed out a stack of pictures of those families and their children.

On December 7, 2003, while America remembered Pearl Harbor Day, I visited an Imam friend of mine and his family. I had in my stack of pictures a photo of his family, so I pulled out the stack and shuffled through them to find it. However, the family members were more interested in looking at all of the other pictures, asking constantly as they would view a new picture, "Who is this?" Then they would all comment on the quality of the picture—not the paper or the color, but on the faces of the people in the pictures.

It was fascinating to watch this little exercise as everyone took part. They would say, "Look at this person, she has a pure face" or "Who is this? His eyes are not honest."

They spent half an hour feasting on the pictures, and continued to ask me who these people were. I watched and marveled as they kept returning to one picture I had of Mrs. Janet Kassup. My Imam friend's mother would ask over and over, "Who is this person? Is she Iraqi? She can't be Iraqi. Is she American?" Then holding the picture so that her son and daughter could both see, she would say, "What a pure face and spirit she has." Then she would turn back to me, "Who is she? Is she Iraqi?"

As I mentioned, Janet Kassup and her family are the one Christian family among that little community on Janain. They do radiate and shine differently than the rest. From the pictures, our conversation turned to Christmas, and out of the blue, I was asked to explain the meaning of the Christmas tree. The Imam's sister, Abir, offered, "Is it the meaning that Christ was born in Bethlehem?"

I thought a moment, and then told them that there are several versions of what the Christmas tree stands for, but for me, it represents the Tree of Life which our first parents were allowed to freely eat of while in the Garden of Eden.

A sudden hush came over my friends, and then almost as though on cue, they all chimed in, "The story of the apple and Eve being blamed for the punishment of Adam is not true."

I agreed with them, and said that I also did not believe that Eve was to blame for Adam's decision to eat. But rather, I believed that Adam needed Eve to better understand why he had to eat. I told them that Adam could not have done it without her, and that in our Bible, God never asked, "Why?" He instead asked, "Where and who?"

"Adam, where art thou?" (Gen 3:9) God knew WHERE Adam was physically or geographically. He was still in the garden, in His holy presence, and had no other place to go at that point. The Lord wanted Adam to know, however, WHERE he was, both spiritually and temporally. Adam had just chosen to transgress a law, and would as a result be separated from God's presence.

> *Who told thee that thou wast naked?*
> —Genesis 3:11

The Lord also knew Adam was naked, and had been from the beginning, but Adam did not know that. Suddenly nakedness became an issue. I have pondered and troubled over this simple question much of my life. Why suddenly did their nakedness become important enough to mention?

My Muslim friend and his family were very quiet and intent on listening to every word I spoke. I suggested that God wanted to see if Adam knew where his heart was, and whether or not he could see the simple yet naked truth of his situation. I suggested that Adam merely honored his wife when he replied to God, but took full responsibility for his actions.

I told them, "When I see a Christmas tree, I see the Tree of Life, and as a Christian, it represents Jesus Christ and His love for all of us."

After a few moments of silence, the Imam said, slowly and softly, "What you say is the truth! It is so very true that Adam and Haoua (Eve) freely ate of that Tree of Life while in the Garden, but afterward were not allowed to eat of it. God protected it, and would not allow Adam to eat anymore from it."

His mother added, "You are a Christian, and we are Muslim, but we believe the very same thing. The truth you speak is in your face and eyes." I paused, and then asked if they remembered that picture of Janet Kassup. They did, and I told them she has Christ in her face also. I said, "Janet has that light which you recognize as pure and good. It is the Light of Christ. Everyone has it, but not all of us have it as bright as others."

There was another pause, and then Abir said, "Oh, Chaplain Tony, we love you. You are sent to us by the God, and you have blessed us and our family. We thank the God for you, and pray always that the God will protect and defend you."

What power there is in such a simple image!

Alma was teaching some of his brethren who were struggling in living the gospel of Jesus Christ and blaming their troubles on others. He asked this simple question:

> And now behold, I ask of you, my brethren of the church, have ye spiritually been born of God? Have ye received his image in your countenances? Have ye experienced this mighty change in your hearts?
>
> —Alma 5:14

I thought and pondered on that experience, and the impact it had on me. I was humbled and filled with gratitude that I had a knowledge and understanding that those people didn't. Yet they understood and knew enough to recognize and appreciate what they saw and felt.

Throughout my career and even my life, people have approached me and commented on that different light or appearance about me that stands out.

But never had I experienced this like I did in Iraq. Each day, Iraqis would single me out and comment on my appearance. They'd say, "There is something different about you" or "Your light is brighter." I heard many different versions of this same concept. Interestingly enough, some time ago, I decided to write a personal mission statement. This statement defines me, and gives clarity to who I want to become, and how I will do so.

My mission statement has evolved from a long full-blown military mission statement to a simple statement: "Having His image engraven in my countenance."

I had struggled with this mission statement. Nothing I would write seemed to hit the target. I felt good about much of it, yet after writing it, I realized that it wasn't what I really wanted. Not until I had arrived at this mission statement did I ever really have peace concerning it. Then one day while I was reading the Book of Alma, it hit me. *This is it!* I want more than anything to have His image in my countenance. To have the image of God engraven in my countenance would equate to being one with Him. It answers everything else about me I want answered.

I often ponder my mission statement and actually strive to achieve it daily. Personally, I feel that I still have far to go, but when bombarded constantly by Iraqis wanting to know why I am different, I have determined that I am on track, and not doing nearly as badly as I often think I am. Perhaps it is this constant feeling of being off track that keeps me constantly reviewing my progress and struggling to remain on track.

When I was younger, I often thought of that question Alma posed to his dissenting brethren. I expected it would be a single event that would occur in one's life. So I waited for that time to come, always looking forward to it. But I have learned that it is not an event nearly as much as it is a process consisting of many mini-events. If "event" were used to define this change that comes over a person, then the event happens multiple times daily, and at times this event looks like a setback or failure, while at times takes on the appearance of success.

The commandment Christ gave to "Be ye therefore perfect, even as your Father which is in Heaven is perfect" (Matt 5:48) is the command form of the same event that Alma poses in the form of a question when he asked, "Have ye received His image in your countenances?" (Alma 5:14)

To be fulfilled and to possess His image in your countenance is the outcome of silent and daily submission to conforming to His will over our own. We will wake up one day and people will notice the difference. They'll say, "You are different. What is it?"

John spoke of this change that all of the worthy saints of God would experience. This change would be life-transforming, and would make everyone who experienced become better people.

> Beloved, now are we the sons of God, and it doth not yet appear what we shall be: but we know that, when he shall appear, we shall be like him; for we shall see him as he is.
>
> And every man that hath this hope in him purifieth himself, even as he is pure.
>
> —1 John 3:2-3

The thought that everyone can have His image within our own countenance is humbling. The prophet Joseph's description of the Father and the Son are that they looked the same. The thought of having a look, an appearance and even a likeness of Him whose name I have taken upon myself inspires me.

My experience in Iraq has changed how I approach my baptismal covenant, and how I view the significance of taking the name of Jesus Christ upon myself. I can no longer ignore how that single event, my baptism, has direct application to all that I think, feel, and do. People are looking intently into my face, seeing the light that burns there. For some there will be a bit of confusion as to what that light is, but to others will come an immediate recognition.

On one occasion while visiting my families in Janain, I ran into a man who claimed to be neither Christian nor Muslim. Instead, he told me he led a group that followed the teachings of John the Baptist. He had my attention! I had to learn more about this man and his group. He invited me down to the Tigress River to meet with members of his congregation and to learn more about their religion.

The distance wasn't far, and in a few minutes I was standing along the Tigress, surrounded by people all dressed in white robes. Men and women alike were dressed in white, and priests were conducting baptisms in the "living water" of the Tigress.

I stayed for quite a while and had a wonderful time watching the baptisms and speaking with these gentle, kind people. They accepted me among them and my heart was touched by their loving ways.

After the morning's baptisms, their priests invited me to their temple down the road to meet with their high priest. I was of course excited by this opportunity to learn more about a people I had never been aware of before.

When I walked into the office of the high priest, I was struck with a sense of familiarity. On the wall behind his desk was a painting of a large white cross, draped with a white robe, and a green wreath of olive leaves sitting on top, with a dove descending down. It grabbed my attention.

It was obvious to me what the imagery stood for, but I wanted to hear what they had to say about it. The priest was quick to point out that there was no cross in the picture, but rather a stand to display the robe. But I clearly saw a cross and instantly thought of the words:

The voice of him that crieth in the wilderness, Prepare ye the way of the LORD, make straight in the desert a highway for our God.

—Isaiah 40:3

I could see in the eyes of this high priest a different light. It was brighter than my Muslim friends, but not nearly as bright as the light in Janet Kassup's eyes.

We talked a long time, and during the conversation, the high priest mentioned a few times that I looked like a messenger from God. He said that he could see God in my face and wanted to know more about what I believed. His eyes were searching for some link between his beliefs and mine. He asked what I thought about John the Baptist, and at the same time he assured me that it was John that baptized Jesus Christ, and that they were cousins.

I sat listening and praying about what I might say or do that would plant the appropriate seeds in the minds and hearts of the men sitting in that office. They explained how they purposely performed their baptisms in the current—or "living water"—the part of the river that carried the "life."

I suddenly felt I should share with them what I knew of John the Baptist, so I started with the "living water" of the Susquehanna River near Harmony, Pennsylvania on May 15, 1829. I told them how Joseph Smith and Oliver Cowdery received a visit from John the Baptist and were both given the Aaronic Priesthood. They were then instructed by John to baptize each other in the river. I told them that John was sent to those two men by Jesus Christ, and that through this visit John the Baptist did the same thing he did anciently—he prepared the way for the gospel of Jesus Christ.

As soon as I said this the priests all came off their seats. The room exploded with chatter—a mix of Arabic and broken English. I was peppered with questions such as,

"What is that you say? How did John appear? Was he a ghost? When and where did this happen? Tell us more! Are you sure about this?"

The high priest grabbed my hand and said, "You are a messenger from God, and have been sent to us. We welcome you here. No other American or outsider has been in our temple. You are the first, and I ask you to be our friend. You must come to us every week and speak to us."

They were hungry to know more about their beloved John the Baptist, and I was grateful for the opportunity to meet these genuine, humble people. Their faces were pure and happy. I could see that they had suffered dearly from the oppression of Saddam Hussein's regime, but they were an industrious and happy people, governed by the same strict laws the Lord gave Moses in the wilderness.

My time spent with this group was eye-opening as I witnessed how the Lord is preparing the way for the gospel of Jesus Christ to truly reach all people.

One Sunday morning, I visited a congregation of Chaldeans called the John the Baptists. They met near the Tigress River in the shade of a highway bridge. They are not Arab, but are descendants of the original Iraqis. They claim to follow the religion taught by John the Baptist.

*Here the priest is finding a suitable spot for that
morning's baptisms.*

*Next the priest begins the process of preparing the "living water"
of the Tigress River for the baptisms.*

The person receiving the baptism begins by washing his face and positioning himself behind and to the right of the priest.

The priest then washes the person in preparation for the immersion.

The person then immerses himself three times.

Once the person has completed his own immersion, he approaches the priest, who then says a prayer over him and immerses him once again. The baptisms are performed for men, women, and older children.

A few members of the group eagerly gather as they wait their turns to be baptized.

One of the priests is making a ring out of olive twigs and leaves. After the baptisms, the people are given rings by the priests to put on their fingers as a symbol of peace.

One of the priests, joined by his sons.
They are friendly, peaceful people.

Here I am in a photo with several members of the group.
I felt right at home with them.

The baptismal service is also a time to share a meal.
They spread out their blankets and enjoy each other's company.

This little old lady wanted to feed me, which is a symbol of respect and acceptance in their culture. I was in!

Here are some of the wonderful women in the group. They each exhibited a calmness and sense of peace that was in contrast to the wartime circumstances that surrounded them and their countrymen.

I later visited the priests of the John the Baptists in their temple. As we talked, there were fifteen priests in the room, and they all came off their seats when I told them John the Baptist had visited Joseph Smith and Oliver Cowdery near Pennsylvania's Susquehanna River in 1829. They had to know more about such a fantastic story—so I told them! In this photo, one of the chief priests is reading to me from their Book of Adam, a book that they consider to be scripture. They believe that both Abraham and John the Baptist taught from this ancient book.

This mural is in the center of their temple's main room and stands as a symbol of their religion. It depicts John the Baptist baptizing Jesus Christ, with a dove landing on the staff. In the left side of this photo you can see a portion of a glass case. This case contains a cross, a white silk robe and an olive wreath. The white robe symbolizes what happens to the souls of those who are baptized— they are washed clean.

CHAPTER FIVE

FORSAKE YOUR NETS AND STRAIGHTWAY FOLLOW HIM...

I met an Iraqi man who embodied an important principle and managed to teach me an important lesson. Initially, he approached me after a council meeting I attended and said, "You are a man of God, and you have come to my country with a message from the God. Please help me. My daughter has no hearing and I need you to help her."

After seven months of living in Iraq, I had grown a bit tired of being approached by Iraqis begging and pleading for money, food, and medicine. I had given approximately $2,000 of my own money to helping Iraqi families, but something about this man captured my attention and sparked an interest.

I saw there was something different in his eyes. Light illuminated his entire being, and I felt the strength of his spirit. One day I decided to visit his home and meet his family, and upon doing so, I was overwhelmed with a feeling of love.

He could tell this man loved his wife and each of his children. Life was a gift God had graciously given him, and he intended to live it according to the will of God.

Nearly eleven years earlier, this man was a young lieutenant serving in Saddam Hussein's army in the southern part of Iraq. Ironically, about the same time he was walking the ground of the southern portion of Iraq near Saudi Arabia and Kuwait, I was assigned to Riyadh, Saudi Arabia, as an Air Defense Liaison Officer to the Joint Forces Air Commander.

On a couple of occasions during that time, I was able to ride as a passenger in an Air Force AWACS—the big 707 aircraft with the large disc on top—flying high above the border of Iraq as we looked out over the horizon with our powerful radar for any possible air threats.

During those flights I often thought about Moses and the children of Israel wandering around in the wilderness for forty years. I also thought of Abraham beginning his journey from Ur, in the land of the Chaldeans.

I then thought about the possible future of Iraq and the people possibly having the restored gospel of Jesus Christ taken to them. I remember a feeling that the Lord would have me back in due time, and perhaps even in Iraq.

It is interesting that during those flights, this same Iraqi man was living in the very area over which I flew.

Evidently, at this same time a couple of Bedouins had crossed the border of Saudi Arabia into Iraq and were captured by this man's unit. He was given orders from his leader to execute the men.

But his conscience wouldn't allow him to kill them. The Bedouins were innocent of any crimes other than not recognizing any boundaries or borders—they only wanted to herd their goats and camels. This Iraqi man was then taken prisoner by Saddam's secret military police and tortured with electricity and various other implements of torture. Today, he wears the scars of burnt flesh from the shocks he received from his fellow countrymen.

His fingers were put in vices and crushed slowly under great pressure. He was beaten with sticks and leather straps, and repeatedly asked why he disobeyed the order to execute those men. His answer was always defiant and bold as he claimed he could not offend God in such a way. This only served to fuel the anger and hatred his captors held for him.

Somehow my friend managed to eventually escape, and by using his training he evaded the secret police of Saddam's regime for several years.

I asked him what had kept him going while in prison. His response inspired me. He said, "I knew that God was watching over me, and I didn't dare do anything to make Him angry with me. I knew that God's wrath would be more fierce than anything those men did to me."

With a broad smile, he told me how he had learned to hide and earn money to both survive and get to his wife and daughter so they could also survive. He told me of the many blessings he had received from God, and how he knew that God had preserved him for something important. He felt God had called him, and that calling required an empty net. So today in Iraq, this man lives humbly, reunited at last with his family, and as a free man.

But as he said, he carries no net, and wastes no time over the past horrors he has had to endure. His focus is on what God needs from him, which at this point is to bless the lives of others less fortunate than he is by using the trades he had to learn while running from his captors. Among other things, he is a plumber, an electrician, a boat pilot, a fisherman, a welder, and a mason.

I have visited the many families living in his area and seen his handiwork firsthand. Most families are less fortunate than him, and he helps them for free. He sees it as an opportunity to give back to God what he feels God has given him.

I learned that sorrow, hardship and trials are not

worthy of my attention or focus. Surviving may require my attention, but survival without the presence and influence of the Lord's Spirit is not possible. At best, all we can do is manage to postpone the inevitable.

Ultimately, we all will need to come to terms with the truth of life, which truth cannot be separated from the Lord. We either align ourselves with Him and live under the umbrella of His light and love, or we venture out and struggle with constantly having to mend our nets to hold onto whatever vice and compulsion we are most fond of.

I will relate a lesson I learned prior to deploying to Iraq. In pondering my assignment to serve the Lord as a chaplain in the Army, I read the story of the Lord calling Peter, James and John to the ministry. He gave a simple invitation: "Follow me, and I will make you fishers of men."

Matthew's version of the story says that "they straightway left their nets and followed Him."

Mark's version says that they "straightway they forsook their nets, and followed him." (Mark 1:18)

> And Jesus, walking by the sea of Galilee, saw two brethren, Simon called Peter, and Andrew his brother, casting a net into the sea: for they were fishers.
>
> And he saith unto them, Follow me, and I will make you fishers of men.
>
> And they straightway left their nets, and followed him.
>
> And going on from thence, he saw other two brethren, James the son of Zebedee, and John his brother, in a ship with Zebedee their father, mending their nets; and he called them.
>
> And they immediately left the ship and their father, and followed him.
>
> —Matthew 4:18-22

I have grown to love this story, as it is an example to me of how I must ultimately approach my callings and stewardships within the Lord's kingdom. I have often thought of the powerful statement made by the great Lamanite king, the father of King Lamoni, as he spoke with Aaron. He asked:

> *What shall I do that I may have this eternal life of which thou hast spoken? Yea, what shall I do that I may be born of God, having this wicked spirit rooted out of my breast, and receive his Spirit, that I may be filled with joy, that I may not be cast off at the last day? Behold, said he, I will give up all that I possess, yea, I will forsake my kingdom, that I may receive this great joy.*
>
> *O God, Aaron hath told me that there is a God; and if there is a God, and if thou art God, wilt thou make thyself known unto me, and I will give away all my sins to know thee,*
>
> —Alma 22: 15,18

What shall we then do? The answer is found in the forsaking of our nets. As we drop our nets, we will find that the Lord will provide for us in all of our needs.

This, however is our greatest challenge—the forsaking of and complete dropping of our sins, our compulsive behaviors, our natural perceptions, and our attitudes. Essentially this is anything that takes us away from the light and presence of the Lord, or distracts our attention from what He wants us to focus on. These things are all neatly contained within the nets that we each carry around with us. Like a security blanket, our nets contain our comfort zones, addictions, bad habits and unique perceptions that enable us to feel justified in seeing the world any other way than through the eyes of the Lord.

During my study of this call that the Lord extended to

his disciples, I was drawn to the question the Lord asked Peter along the shore of the Sea of Tiberias on the morning of His third visit to them after His resurrection.

As I read through that story, my attention was drawn to the fish. On the shore, the Lord had a fire kindled and had prepared fish and bread for them. Yet in the net was an astounding 153 fish, freshly caught by Peter and those that were with him. The Lord instructed them to bring ashore the fish which they had caught, and Peter complied. After they had dined, the Lord turned to Peter and asked:

> *Simon, son of Jonas, lovest thou me more than these? He saith unto him, Yea, Lord; thou knowest that I love thee. He saith unto him, Feed my lambs.*
>
> —John 21:15

Suddenly, a question formed in my mind. Who was the Lord referring to when He asked, "Lovest thou me more than these?"

The Lord asked this question three times, and Peter grew more perplexed each time. Was the Lord speaking of those that went fishing with him? Or, is it possible that the reference to "these" were the fish contained within the nets which Peter and his friends had just taken back up?

Three years earlier, a simple invitation was extended and humbly answered. Yet somehow Peter had forgotten the complete and total commitment that was required of him when he initially answered that call by "dropping" or "forsaking" his nets in order to "straightway follow Him."

One of my frustrations in Iraq was keeping LDS soldiers motivated to live true and faithfully to their covenants and obligations as members of the Lord's Kingdom here on earth. I have seen strong members lose testimonies and all interest in partaking of the sacrament as they allowed the "fish" in their nets to become their prize and sole attention.

Some simply lost their focus on the Lord's Kingdom as they paid more attention to the items in the nets they carried around with them. In this particular story, Peter returned to his nets and had fished all the night long without catching anything.

How true it is with us even today. We enter into the Kingdom of the Lord with enthusiasm, but somewhere along the way we lose just enough of that excitement to allow our attention to return to our old nets and what we carry in them.

Separation is again the focus here, as Peter and all of us find it difficult to separate ourselves from our own ways. It is this separation—or lack of it—that prevents us from growing closer to the Lord and increasing our spiritual zeal and might. On one hand, we separate ourselves from our nets to latch onto the Spirit of the Lord and His law, which leads us to happiness. We experience a new way of being, and all of the blessings that come as a result of the inner change.

On the other hand, if we leave the light of truth and return to our old nets, we separate ourselves from the testimony gained and from the small portion of the Lord's Spirit that we have obtained.

SIMPLY LETTING GO

I cannot count the times soldiers have told me that they cannot "let go" of whatever troubles them. Addiction, compulsion, anger, jealousy, hate, guilt, sorrow—you name it. When something becomes controlling, it is not that easy to simply let go. But letting go of the vice or troubling compulsion is only half of the struggle. Learning to let go of the emotions that accompany them is just as troubling.

One soldier in great sorrow told me that he deeply

regretted committing adultery. Being in Iraq for nearly a year has helped him to overcome the desire to be unfaithful, and it has strengthened his resolve to be faithful. But the guilt and feelings of depression that accompany any memory of his bad choice quickly fill him with despair and hopelessness. His wife struggles with trusting him again, and has trouble believing that he is truly repentant. She cannot let go of the powerful emotions attached to the memory of betrayal.

I have come to believe that for those who suffer in this manner do so needlessly. The Lord has promised that if we come unto Him and repent of our sins, we can avoid suffering.

> *For behold, I, God, have suffered these things for all, that they might not suffer if they would repent;*
>
> *But if they would not repent they must suffer even as I;*
> —Doctrine and Covenants 19:16-17

How do we sufficiently repent of our sins to receive the tremendous blessing of not having to suffer? By simply letting go of them. Forsaking sins is nothing more than developing a desire and taste for righteousness, and choosing to sin no more.

To the woman brought before Him who supposedly was caught in adultery, the Lord asked,

> *Woman, where are those thine accusers? hath no man condemned thee?*
> —John 8:10

> *She replied, No man, Lord. And Jesus said unto her, Neither do I condemn thee: go, and sin no more.*
> —John 8:11

How is it done? How do we simply go and sin no more? How do we let go of our inner conflicts, feelings of inadequacy, and lack of self-worth? How do we simply choose to be different when inside we cannot let go of whatever takes our minds and hearts away from God and His Great and matchless Spirit?

I believe for many of us, such a feat will require great tears of sorrow and a tremendous inner resolve to become different than we currently are. By simply turning to the Lord in heartfelt sincere prayer, we can at least begin the process of letting go.

Through such prayer, we can begin to empty our minds and hearts of the prevailing thoughts that prevent us from feeling and experiencing the Spirit of the Lord.

We have to first want to let go, then in mighty prayer, we should ask the Lord to help us successfully let go by giving us sufficient portions of His Spirit to enable us to continue in our determination to become different creatures.

We must take inventory of our nets. Recognize that in order to serve the Lord, we must leave our nets behind, and all that they carry. To be truly successful in this effort, we must decide to let go of our nets completely, without condition. We must draw upon the Lord's abundant love and strength to help us bless the lives of those around us.

Early one day a man from Uganda, Africa, came to see me. We were in Wiesbaden, Germany, and this man needed to talk. He felt so far from home and deeply missed his parents. This man had a hunger for God's Spirit, and wanted to feast on His word. He asked if I had anything he could read that would help him feel closer to God. "Of course I do," I thought to myself.

I asked him if he had a Bible, to which he replied he did. But he wanted something more, as he sensed there had to be something more. I handed him a Book of Mormon and bore my testimony of it and the powerful teachings of Christ it contained. He dropped his head and lowered his eyes, telling me that he could not accept that book. His father had warned him of it and made him promise not to touch it.

He felt the presence of the Spirit as I shared my humble testimony of the book to him, yet he could not even hold it in his hands. I inquired why he couldn't, especially after asking me for something more and feeling the presence of the Spirit concerning the book. He responded, "I feel it must be true, and has to contain more of God's word, but I have given my promise to my father and cannot break that. I will just have to be satisfied with what I have until my father changes his mind."

I was struck by the force of this young man's integrity and honesty. I was humbled and quite touched by his response. All I could do was marvel at his love and devotion to his father. How I wished I could be like him. How I wish I could stand in the face of temptation or any distraction that separates me from His Spirit, and always say, "I cannot even touch it, for my Father has made me promise, and I cannot break my promise."

CHAPTER SIX

LET YOUR LIGHT SO SHINE...

My first Sunday in Iraq, I was asked to go to the Baghdad Airport and pick up a Catholic priest and bring him back to the Green Zone for our Catholic soldiers. My assistant, a little angry that I made him drive, commented that it would be his luck that if we got hit on our trip, I'd get killed and he would survive. He wanted me to explain how he would explain that. (Most chaplain assistants are programmed in their schooling to be bodyguards for their defenseless chaplains. I broke that paradigm a bit, since I refused to have a bodyguard.)

We were just leaving the compound of our palace, and stopped at the guard gate. I was telling him that I work for God, and not to worry. I said, "If the Lord needs me on the other side of the veil, I'm ready to go. If not, I'll be perfectly safe."

At that moment we heard a very large explosion. Not more than thirty seconds down the road from us, a car bomb exploded. Had we not stopped at the guard gate for those short moments, we would have been caught in the blast area, and perhaps killed. As we drove by the burning car and debris, I turned to my assistant and said with a smile, "I guess He still wants us down here."

This particular kind of thing happened with frequency in Iraq. My assistant and those closest to me would marvel, yet they knew that the Lord was involved directly with my ministry and my life. I simply enjoyed the journey and the adventure, trying to shine the light of my testimony whenever and wherever possible.

> *Ye are the light of the world. A city that is set on an hill cannot be hid.*
>
> *Neither do men light a candle, and put it under a bushel, but on a candlestick; and it giveth light unto all that are in the house.*
>
> *Let your light so shine before men, that they may see your good works, and glorify your Father which is in heaven.*
> —Matthew 5:14-16

This is one of those little things that has always been on my mind—letting my light so shine, as opposed to letting the Lord's light so shine. In nearly all of the references in the scriptures, any light referred to is that of the Lord's light. Yet, the Lord instructed those early saints in Jerusalem that they had to learn to let "their" light so shine.

We believe that every human born into this mortal existence has woven in the fabric of their being the Light of Christ, which light leads us to truth.

The Psalmist noted that the Word of the Lord is a lamp and lights our path.

> *Thy word is a lamp unto my feet, and a light unto my path.*
> —Psalms 119:105

The Savior testified of himself to those ancient saints that He was the light of the world.

> *Then spake Jesus again unto them, saying, I am the light of the world: he that followeth me shall not walk in darkness, but shall have the light of life.*
> —John 8:12

To those ancient saints on the American continent, the Lord testified of himself:

> *Behold, I am the law, and the light. Look unto me, and endure to the end, and ye shall live; for unto him that endureth to the end will I give eternal life.*
> —3 Nephi 15:9

Given this truth, Jesus is the Light of the World, yet He told the ancient saints on both continents to hold up "their" light, and to let it shine.

During His visit to the American saints He added that He was that light which they were to hold up.

> *Therefore, hold up your light that it may shine unto the world. Behold I am the light which ye shall hold up—that which ye have seen me do.*
> —3 Nephi 18:24

Now this has been a topic of much thought and consideration. I have often wondered why the Lord, who spoke clearly and did not mix words, spoke of two lights, yet only meant one. Or possibly two different sources can provide this "one" light.

One morning while I spoke to my battalion commander, he revealed a lesson learned while executing a judgment over a soldier that had violated the law. He told me of a feeling that he had inside that compelled him to ask his company commanders a certain question. However, the answer to the question didn't satisfy that inner voice. He decided to yield to that inner voice and insist that his company commanders dig deeper and research their answers more. Each came back and admitted that they had given the wrong information earlier, and that after researching the matter, new information was required to be given.

I asked the commander if he had learned anything. He

thought a moment, and then replied that he had learned to be more thorough. I stopped him and suggested that he really learned to pay attention to that inner voice, or light illuminating his path to truth.

Herein is our dance step with the Spirit. We receive either a flicker of light illuminating the path to truth, or we get that and the enticings of the Holy Ghost. In the instant that we pay attention to that light and the enticings of the Spirit, we HONOR the Spirit, the Lord, ourselves, and those with whom we are dealing with. This honoring process takes on the form of righteousness as we are basically following the inner stirrings of the Lord and moving in the direction He wants us to move in. We become more honorable, which is a foundation of character, and engenders honor in those around us. Faithfulness is another attribute we integrate into our character in this process of honoring the Light of Christ and the enticings of the Holy Spirit.

This honoring process is the process of "continuing in His word" which process illuminates our path with the light of truth, setting us free or liberating us from consequences that betraying that inner sense brings. (John 8:31-32) It also can bring the liberation of past mistakes and betraying choices by setting our feet on the correct path of change and perfection.

> That which is of God is light; and he that receiveth light, and continueth in God, receiveth more light; and that light groweth brighter and brighter until the perfect day.
>
> And again, verily I say unto you, and I say it that you may know the truth, that you may chase darkness from among you;
>
> —Doctrine & Covenants 50:24-25

I have seen the Light of Christ in the faces of many people of all races and from different countries as they strive to live their lives correctly, in accordance to that inner light given to them at their birth.

I had a soldier struggling with anger and feelings of being segregated and unfairly treated by the command. After spending several hours counseling with him, and not feeling like I had made any headway with him, I suggested to the command that he be my driver for a week. I felt that by spending a week with me, and experiencing everything I do in the course of a week, he would have a new perspective from which to view his surroundings and circumstances.

After the first day, this solder was cracking infrequent smiles, of which I was quick to make note of. By the second day, this solder was smiling with greater frequency and even laughing on occasion.

By the end of our third day together, this angry and rough soldier was asking questions and even participating in conversations with local Iraqis. His smile lit up his face, and transformed this hardened young man to the point that Iraqi people began to comment on his light.

One stop we made was at the home of an Iraqi guard. This man had four beautiful children. His oldest daughter, who was eleven years old, had the most attracting and magnetic smile I've seen. My angry soldier was taken by her charm and light.

When we left that home all he could talk about was how that little girl glowed. I stopped him momentarily, looked him in the eyes, and told him that when he smiled and had genuine concern for others, he glowed with equal brightness and was virtually a different man.

His anger and bitterness all seemed to instantly dissipate,

and that new perspective suddenly came to light and a permanent change seemed to come over him.

This same soldier got to visit several of the families in that small community I had adopted where all of the families are Muslim with the exception of the Chaldean Catholic family. I deliberately took him from home to home, walking in and visiting each family. By the time we visited the Christian family, he turned to me and commented, "This is strange. I feel something different here. This family is the most loving and different family I've ever seen in Iraq. There is definitely something special here."

I remember the first time I visited that family when I first arrived to Iraq. It was hot, and my work days were long. Walking into their home was like walking out of the combat zone I was in and momentarily taking refuge in a place where a greater abundance of the Spirit of the Lord resided.

This family has struggled tremendously under the former regime, and now face ever-changing prejudice and religious posturing. They are isolated and feel so very helpless against the backdrop of Islamic influence all around them.

One night I visited them, taking along my laptop computer and my *Finding Faith in Christ* DVD. Although their English is a bit rough, they all gathered around the screen and amidst tears and gasps of breath they all consumed the images they saw. The father periodically would kiss his fingers and then touch the screen. The mother would clasp her hands, and with tears streaming down her cheeks, simply sat in silent wonder.

When scripture was spoken, they would all look at each other and recite the same scripture in Aramaic, which is the language they speak in their home.

After the movie ended we spoke at length about that

thing that distinguished them from everyone else in Iraq—that light of Christ that glows brighter and demands greater faithfulness and obedience to it. They understood, and seemed grateful for the time we spent with them.

One another occasion, along with my angry soldier, we visited them to find everyone disturbed and emotionally upset. The women were all crying and angry, and the men were beside themselves with anger. One of the daughters had been accused of stealing a very large sum of money from another family in the community. I sat and listened to them argue their plight, and I felt their sorrow. Of course, the girl accused was innocent, but could not prove it. They pleaded with me to do something and to help them find peace.

During the war, they and everyone in the community had to evacuate their homes as that community was heavily bombed by coalition bombers. By the time everyone returned to their homes, they all found them stripped of everything they possessed. "Ali Baba," the common term for thief, had quickly come in to the community and stolen everything of worth, everything but the walls and roof.

All of the families in the community went out and found several buildings that had been vacated and did unto them as they had been done unto. They looted and pillaged for furniture and what ever they could find useful or profitable—everyone, that is, except this sole Christian family that lived in their midst. The men of the community would approach them and tell them that they would have to hurry to get what they needed before coalition troops shut down access to the building being looted.

Akram, the father of this humble Christian family, would refuse on the grounds that it was not right, and that God would frown on them for doing it. So, everyone in the community had furniture, and various items stolen out of the buildings they looted, except Akram and his family.

Now they struggled in the wake of this accusation that their daughter had stolen money.

As I sat in their home and felt their anguish, I told them that they had to take courage and to learn to love these people even in the midst of false accusations. Christ's gospel demanded of them to continue to live according to their belief, and not waver. Slapping myself on one cheek, I told them that Christ taught to turn the other cheek and to love and bless those that accuse us, and that such storms of trial are given to establish God's truth in greater ways.

I testified to them that their refusal to steal and loot along with the other families would be their testimony of innocence and would rebuke those making the accusations. They all knew they were honest, and could not live in deceit or sin.

I checked up on them the next night after Sunday services, and offered to kneel down and pray with them as a family. A special spirit was present as I prayed, and the family all seemed to be strengthened somehow, knowing that God was in fact pleased with their choices and sacrifices in order to live correctly.

I marvel at the thought of how difficult life must be not knowing that God lives, and that His Son Jesus Christ is in fact a resurrected being leading and guiding His church on the earth today. This little family of Chaldean Catholics in the midst of Muslims is indeed a bright light and influence for good. They do not know it, nor really recognize that their efforts to live in accordance with their faith has had an impact on those around them. I prayed that the hearts of those around them would soften to the good news of the everlasting gospel of Jesus Christ, and that those good people in Iraq would recognize the restored truth and the need to embrace it.

This is Janet Kassup. She and her family are the only Christians in the little community on Janain. She truly radiates a special spirit of love. She is like a rock for the other women in her neighborhood. They rely upon her for strength and support.

This little treasure is Sema, Janet Kassup's granddaughter. We had invited their family to take a tour of the great palace that now serves as the Coalition Provisional Headquarters.

A happy reunion in Iraq with my youngest brother, Pete. We had not seen each other for nearly ten years. I was able to spend several days with him. Pete flies the Army's Kiowa 58D, and on several occasions he would fly over my location to let me know he was there covering me.

Pete and I take a rest after a long day of working on aircraft. He tried to instruct me on all of the intricacies of the aircraft he flies. I did my best to just keep up with him, but as you can see, I was dragging.

I often felt the Lord's guidance in reuniting family members. It seems I was always able to be in the right place at just the right moment to get people together. On this occasion, I was able to locate the cousin of one of the pilots in my brother's unit. These young men hadn't seen each other for quite some time, and it was a boost to their spirits.

WATCH AND PRAY

When the Savior entered the Garden of Gethsemane, He stopped at the entrance and posted his faithful disciples there. He then instructed them to "pray lest they enter into temptation."

> *And when he was at the place, he said unto them, Pray that ye enter not into temptation.*
> —Luke 22:40

Throughout my life I have been brought back to this statement and compelled to think deeply on what the Savior was teaching those disciples. What temptation did they need to avoid? And how would praying help them avoid it?

On returning to his disciples after his own initial prayer within the Garden, He found them sleeping. Upon awakening them, he gently chastened them.

> *And said unto them, Why sleep ye? rise and pray, lest ye enter into temptation.*
> —Luke 22:46

Now sleep has entered into the equation. How often am I found asleep while posted guard and given stewardship and responsibility to serve and minister to others. I think of Home Teaching assignments that I have slept through, or sons and daughters growing up while I slept, missing out on much of the joy and blessings of their youth. How about the many other assignments and responsibilities in and out of the Church that I have missed because I slept?

Those disciples were tired. They had been up many hours, and had eaten a large dinner with the Master just shortly before being going to the Garden. Sleep beckoned, taunting them, and they succumbed.

I have learned throughout my life and ministry that

prayer is a powerful tool to help me keep my vision clear and my focus sharp. It is the Spirit of the Lord that I am charged to carry with me at all times—not just periodically, or when it is convenient. The commandment was given after I was baptized, "Receive the Holy Ghost!" Compliance with this commandment is to "let my light so shine before men." I believe that there is light to be seen in my desire and willingness to comply and obey the commandments of the Lord. Somehow, what is seen is the makings of a story that others can relate to and in some way motivate and strengthen them.

Each of us have been given a posting and assignment in the Lord's church. In addition to this, we have accepted postings and assignments as fathers, mothers, sons and daughters, brothers and sisters. These relationships each demand of us to be a certain way, and to shine brightly in the name of truth and the resolve to live it.

The Army teaches all new recruits the first three general orders of the Army, upon which nearly everything in the operation of the Army depends. The first general order is:

> *"I will guard everything within the limits of my post and quit my post only when properly relieved."*
> —Army General Order #1

I've often thought just how pertinent this order is to church service, and in living true and faithfully to my testimony and covenants.

I cannot imagine what shame and inner anxiety must have swelled within Peter's breast when the Lord returned after posting him to watch, only to find him asleep.

The assignment given to Peter did not seem very important. No apparent threat was visible, and without really understanding the assignment, Peter simply gave in to the immediate need to sleep. The Lord said to him:

And he cometh, and findeth them sleeping, and saith unto Peter, Simon, sleepest thou? couldest not thou watch one hour?

Watch ye and pray, lest ye enter into temptation. The spirit truly is ready, but the flesh is weak.
—Mark 14:37-38

As I have pondered this scene, I have felt shame and embarrassment for having to admit that I too have slept at times when charged to watch. Or, if not asleep, I have been distracted by selfish needs and wants. Letting my eye lose sight of the Kingdom of God, and the goal of returning to the presence of the Lord is no different than sleeping while charged to watch.

Letting our light so shine also begins and remains in the decisions we make from moment to moment. Those decisions that determine our focus and occupy our attention also determine the intensity and quality of the light that will emanate from our being.

Verily, verily, I say unto you, ye must watch and pray always, lest ye be tempted by the devil, and ye be led away captive by him.
—3 Nephi 18:15

I have found that the temptation and captivity of the devil is found in those moments that my focus shifts and changes to anything other than my covenants and stewardship in the Lord's church.

When I choose to think, ponder and even behave contrary to what the Spirit of the Lord is enticing me to do, then at that moment and in that thing I so separate myself from the Spirit of the Lord that it has no place in me. It no longer continues to lead me in wisdom's path and prosper and preserve me.

And now, I say unto you, my brethren, that after ye have known and have been taught all these things, if ye should transgress and go contrary to that which has been spoken, that ye do withdraw yourselves from the Spirit of the Lord, that it may have no place in you to guide you in wisdom's paths that ye may be blessed, prospered, and preserved.

—Mosiah 2:36

The Lord's admonition to "pray always lest ye fall into temptation" is really to help us keep our minds and hearts so focused that the Lord's Kingdom is ever at the forefront of each thought, desire, and behavior.

Behold, verily, verily, I say unto you, ye must watch and pray always lest ye enter into temptation; for Satan desireth to have you, that he may sift you as wheat.

—3 Nephi 18:18

As we learn to pray always, asking to see situations and circumstances as the Lord sees them, our perspective changes, and we slowly begin to BE different. Our way of BEING begins to reflect that great, fulfilling light which emanates from the presence of the Lord, even all truth and all light.

Letting "our" light so shine therefore becomes our growing resolve to live for the Lord, rather than ourselves. Living for Him demands a vastly different approach to those we meet, are in relationships with and have stewardships over.

No longer do we become defensive or hurt by words or actions of others. Our focus is on how to better serve and reach even the most difficult of hearts, and we do all of this at the direction and enticing of the Holy Spirit.

My experience in Iraq taught me that the blindness of the mind and heart is perhaps our greatest obstacle and most difficult challenge. In the moment our perception shifts even one degree from the truth, we no longer see truth, but rather a skewed version of it. Soon, that one degree—if gone unchecked—will grow to ten degrees. The farther we move from our point of origin, where truth was still intact, our perception becomes even more skewed, making our sense of reality even more distant from the truth.

Satan makes great use of the tool of deception. He blinds our minds with it, and uses it as a tool to lead us so subtly away from the teachings and truths of the Lord that by the time we recognize them, it seems too late.

Darkness and deception affects our sense of self-worth, our worthiness, and our hope. Wars, bloodshed and thousands of years of hate have been perpetuated and promulgated by the darkness of deception. Men have hated and killed other men because of the darkness of their own deception.

One afternoon I accompanied my battalion commander to the office of a local Iraqi leader. This man and I had engaged in a conversation about truth. It all started when he offered me hot tea. Of course, I declined. He immediately asked, "Why?"

I told him that it was forbidden by my religion. Suddenly he understood, as in his own religion, Islam, there are substances that are forbidden by God. This turned into a conversation that included how people deceive themselves and alter the laws of God. Our conversation progressed, and suddenly we were discussing Zionism, and the problems of America supporting Israel over the Palestinians. I listened as he spoke of the terrible things the Jews had done to the Arab people, and how Muslims suffer as a result of Israel and America's support of it.

With great sincerity, this man told me how all of the lies that have been told about the Jewish people have resulted in America's defense of them.

"What lies?" I asked. He replied, "About the persecution. You know, Hitler and World War II."

He claimed that only about 1,000 Jews were ever killed by Hitler, but the "great fabricated lies" of millions of Jews being killed had made America defend them.

I could not believe a people could be so deeply enmeshed in the deception ploy of the adversary that they could defy history and actually believe something so preposterous and untrue. Yet at the beginning of our conversation, this same man was trying to teach us how mankind changes God's law to meet with man's convenience and lusts.

This blindness of which God's prophets, both past and present, have spoken about is real. It is dangerous, and perhaps even comparable to the very jaws of hell gaping open the mouth wide after each one of us. All Satan needs to accomplish is to skew the truth one degree. We stand on 99 percent truth and don't even recognize the one degree misalignment—at least not at first, and certainly not without the help and guidance of the Spirit.

Comfort, ease, and habit keep us settled in our misaligned way of being, until suddenly something happens in our lives and we discover that we are off the track. Just as suddenly, we realize that correction is not an easy matter, and in this many of us become content with our blindness.

This is much like the story of the missionaries who were proselyting in the Bible belt in the southern United States. As they spoke with an elderly lady who had become comfortable with the anti-Mormon sentiment of the area, she confronted the young Elders on being saved by grace alone. The Elders quickly pointed out that the very Bible she used to support her belief also said that faith without works was dead. Of course this elderly lady could not accept this truth. Her blindness was so complete she simply couldn't let go of her old perceptions to allow for the truth of the Spirit to enter her heart to enlighten her. She immediately denied her Bible said any such thing, and that the Elders must have been mistaking their Mormon Bible with her Bible which contained all of God's word. One of the Elders opened her Bible to the Book of James and read this verse:

> But wilt thou know, O vain man, that faith without works is dead?
>
> —James 2:20

Because the darkness and blindness of this woman was so complete, she immediately tore that page right out of her Bible and then declared, "Like I said, my Bible doesn't say any such thing!"

An experienced Non Commissioned Officer bragged one night in Baghdad at how lucky he was for finalizing a divorce while in theater, and now would be free from having to return home to a bad marriage. Naturally, the counselor in me came out, and I poked around a bit, asking probing questions.

The soldier revealed that he had been married for over eight years, and had suffered greatly during his marriage. Everything he discussed pointed blame on his wife for failing him and his expectations of what a happy marriage should be, but he revealed nothing that seemed she acted out of the normal boundaries of a wife and mother of a young child.

I commented simply, "Give me an hour, and I'll demonstrate that you are really the one who failed the marriage."

Instantly, this struck a nerve, and with emotional guns blazing he defensively lashed back at me, defending his pride and conduct in the marriage. "Believe me, Chaplain, she made me more miserable than you can imagine!" I asked him if he had any idea of how many nights she went to bed with tears because he had neglected her needs, or had failed to provide her with the tenderness and attention she needed from him. Most importantly, how often did she complain that he wasn't who she needed him to be?

Just like the land navigation exercises that I have experienced, departing from a point of origin and allowing for even one degree of error, if gone unchecked that one degree soon grows into many degrees. The further out you go, the greater the error, and consequently the more difficult it is to correct and get back on track.

We become lulled into thinking that all is well, and that our thoughts are harmless, but this is the first degree of error we make. Thoughts turn into desires, which in turn become actions and behavior, which become the monuments we erect to testify either for us, or against us.

> But this much I can tell you, that if ye do not watch yourselves, and your thoughts, and your words, and your deeds, and observe the commandments of God, and continue in the faith of what ye have heard concerning the coming of our Lord, even unto the end of your lives, ye must perish. And now, O man, remember, and perish not.

—Mosiah 4:30

I visited a school one day in Baghdad, and walked into the English class, offering my services to provide conversational English. It was a classroom of girls all about 16 to 17 years of age. With smiles they all greeted me and welcomed the opportunity to speak English.

After about three minutes, however, the conversation turned to a political discussion with many questions, ranging from "Why does America want to be the world police?" to "Where is our oil?"

I quickly realized I had walked into a lion's den, and I was about to be the main course. These girls represented the upper class in Iraq. Their fathers were all Ba'ath Party officers, and were currently out of work. I could imagine the negative and anti-coalition conversations held in their respective homes. In their young faces I saw no light, but rather anger and disillusionment.

In answering their questions as best as I could, I realized that they were so completely blinded to the truth that they actually perceived Saddam Hussein as their loving leader who cared for them and provided the best life they had even known. They were so completely blinded to the truth of his secret prisons, torture chambers and hundreds of thousands of Iraqis that had either been executed or tortured for nothing more than disagreeing with their beloved leader.

I related a story about a mother that approached me one day and begged my help in finding the graves of her two sons. Saddam had them killed just before the war, and now she wanted to know where they were buried. They were good boys, she said, and were only guilty of wanting to stay with their mother instead of guarding a post in downtown Baghdad.

I then asked the girls if they had known of the young female model who had become famous in Iraq before the war. She had been swimming with one of Saddam's sons, and she playfully splashed water in his face. For doing so, he fed her to one of his lions, laughing as he watched her literally get torn to shreds by his starved carnivorous beast.

Of course the girls had not heard of any of these stories. I asked them if they would like to meet the young man, a father of five, who was tortured with electricity and had all of his fingers mashed in a vice for the "crime" of refusing to execute an innocent Kuwaiti Bedouin.

"What proof do you have of any of your unbelievable stories?" one girl asked. Soon we were back to "Where is our oil?" and "Why is our electricity always out?" I asked them if they had ever studied another time in history where a conquering army such as the United States had spent time and resources to pay the opposing forces as we did, or had continued to spend precious blood to establish and defend the new freedom given to those girls and their families.

There was nothing I could say however that would even strike an emotion in the girls. They were so set in their beliefs and understanding that they could not be swayed even one degree.

I decided to change the direction of the conversation to religion. I testified to them that God is watching us, and wants his children to be happy and to have joy. There can never be joy in our lives if we are living contrary to God's wishes or to His plan of Happiness.

"But we were happy before you came!" they all responded. Again, I testified to them that even though they may have felt happy, their seeming happiness came at a tremendous price. Many thousands of their fellow Iraqis had not been happy, nor did they have food, a home, or decent clothes to wear. The opportunity was now placed in each of their laps to reach out and make a great change in Iraq by helping those less fortunate than they were, such as feeding the hungry and recognizing the needs of those without fathers or mothers.

Muslims all believe that there is only one God, and that even the God of Christianity is the same as their God, Allah. I testified to them that God loved them all, whether rich or poor, and that He had led us to their country, and now is guiding us to help rebuild their country. Finally, I didn't receive an argument. They could not dispute that God's apparent will was for America to occupy their country and to give them a new and wonderful gift—freedom.

By the time I walked out of that classroom, I had gained a testimony of the dangers of a blind mind and heart. It is so very real—and dangerous to our ability to recognize and embrace truth. Perhaps this is why the Lord counsels us to be "pure in heart" and to "let virtue garnish our thoughts unceasingly."

> *Let thy bowels also be full of charity towards all men, and to the household of faith, and let virtue garnish thy thoughts unceasingly; then shall thy confidence wax strong in the presence of God; and the doctrine of the priesthood shall distil upon thy soul as the dews from heaven.*
>
> —Doctrine and Covenants 121:45

While walking the halls of the great palace where the Coalition Provisional Authority was based, I ran into an Iraqi man whom I had been introduced to several weeks earlier. This man had grabbed me on a couple of occasions and wanted to know about my religion. He stopped me and asked me if I believed in Joseph Smith and the vision that Joseph claimed to have seen.

I was surprised at his question and wanted to know how he had learned of Joseph Smith. I told this man that not only did I believe in Joseph, but I knew that he actually had seen the vision he claimed to have.

The man couldn't believe it, and thought that God was trying to tell him something, but he couldn't figure out what it was. "That is fantastic," he said. "If it is true, it changes everything in the whole world! How can it be true?"

I asked him how he had learned of Joseph Smith. His reply was that he had heard another chaplain talking about churches in America that are based on lies and deceptions of evil men. Of course, the LDS Church received much of this chaplain's attention. Somehow this sparked an interest in this Iraqi's mind. He had asked himself, "Why would a Christian be so angry and opposed to any church that claims to believe in Christ?"

He had wanted to know more, and consequently got on the internet. I briefly told him the story of the First Vision, and then bore my personal testimony of it. He seemed more interested in my testimony than the actual story itself. "How is it you can know such a thing?" he asked. "Were you there?"

I stopped and in an instant remembered an experience at Fort Jackson, South Carolina. It was the last week of February of 1990. I had been pulling guard duty around the parameter of our bivouac location. I had been praying off and on most of the early morning for a boost to my testimony. I had been separated from my family for several months, and felt so alone and forgotten.

I hurt inside and needed to feel the Lord's love. After my duty, I crawled into my sleeping bag, boots, uniform and all as I only had an hour before revile. As I laid my head on my pillow, I suddenly felt a tremendous force pushing me down and into my cot. So powerful was this force that it prevented me from breathing. I was startled and so completely surprised that I didn't know what to make of it. This powerful sensation that had pushed me down with tremendous force only lasted several seconds, but seemed to last a few minutes.

As soon as it dissipated, I sat up and looked about the tent. A General Purpose Medium Tent holds twenty sleeping soldiers in it. I thought that perhaps someone was playing a prank. After a moment or two of looking and listening for movement, I laid back down.

Suddenly, a second time this powerful force began to push me with even greater weight, making my cot creak under the weight. It lasted a bit longer than the first time, and had my complete attention. I sat up again after it went away, and again looked and listened for any movement, but there was none.

I had a feeling of something very familiar, but couldn't place my finger on it, so I laid back down, eyes wide open. Again, a third time, I was being pushed down into my cot with such great force I thought the cot would break under the weight, and that if it didn't go away soon, I would be smothered to death.

During that third time, I began to remember what was familiar about it, and began to pray with all of my might for help. In an instant, the force was gone, and I was whisked away to a higher vantage point. I looked down and could see young Joseph Smith kneeling on the ground in a grove of trees, looking up into the light of the two personages that appeared to him, even the Father and the Son.

All I was allowed to see was the bright light, but I saw Joseph. For a brief moment, I was allowed by the Spirit to witness firsthand that remarkable event. My heart pounded within my breast and burned with the love of the Lord. I had been given an answer to my prayers, and had been blessed with a knowledge that replaced all faith I had concerning that event. I now *knew* it was true, and could not deny it.

I turned back to my Iraqi friend and simply told him that by the power of the Holy Spirit, he could know the truth of all things. But he would have to think and ponder deeply what it is he was seeking and wanted to know, because once given, he would have a new responsibility to live and become different. He would be expected to be equal to the new knowledge given to him. He would have to change his perception and his whole life.

My Iraqi friend put his hand on my shoulders and told me that God's light was in my eyes, and that it wasn't in the other chaplain's eyes that had spoken badly of my faith. He wanted to know more about the story and again commented on how that story, if true, would change Iraq forever.

A NEW STAR IN THE SKY

And behold, there shall a new star arise, such an one as ye never have beheld; and this also shall be a sign unto you.

—Helaman 14:5

And it came to pass also that a new star did appear, according to the word.

—3 Nephi 1:21

Light really is magical thing. It illuminates, warms, motivates and encourages. Light lifts and inspires the hearts and minds of men while lighting truth's path for us to investigate, and follow. I have often marveled at how it is that some eagerly seek out the light, while others turn from it and choose to live in the darkness which light repels. Even the light from a distant star can provide sufficient illumination to spark hope and encouragement and can even be an answer to prayer.

Christmas in Baghdad came and went with the usual speed that time flies here in the combat zone in Iraq.

At the end of a long Christmas Day, and while driving from one of the units in my battalion, I reflected on my experience of Christmas in Baghdad, separated from my family. With a son in South Africa serving the Lord on a mission, and a daughter, married and living in the United States. My dear wife and other children were living in Germany. Here I sat, in a military vehicle riding along streets marked and scarred by the implements of war.

I pondered what had actually happened on this special day. Lost in thought, reflecting on what Christmas in Baghdad actually was and what it meant to me, I suddenly became aware of a most unusual sight. Directly in front of my vehicle and just above the immediate horizon, a large crescent moon glowed brightly with one lone star resting above the moon. It was awe-inspiring. I had to stop and get out to take a picture of the scene. My mind wandered, and I suddenly could see kings of old, wise men looking up and recognizing the sign given by prophets that the Christ Child was born in the world. Suddenly I knew what Christmas in Baghdad had meant, and what it was that I had actually experienced.

Christmas 2003 in Iraq was an experience I will never forget! Two special days of worship and celebration in a land filled with Christmas history and tradition.

Christmas Eve day began much like any other day in a combat zone. Soldiers stood guard at the checkpoints, and went on patrols. Intelligence estimates had indicated that opposing forces were going to attack Coalition Forces at multiple points simultaneously. The battalion command and staff met for our weekly staff meeting. Soldiers were busy preparing for the attack we anticipated, sensing they were missing out on the tradition of Christmas.

The soldiers of the 40th Engineer Battalion are professionals. No one liked being in Iraq, let alone being here during Christmas away from loved ones, but I watched as the soldiers professionally went about their business without complaining, with a sense of sacrificing something for a greater cause.

Although I was separated from my family on my favorite holiday of the year, I was greatly touched by the sentiment our good soldiers displayed as they honorably did what they were called to do.

During the morning Command and Staff meeting, I played a segment of the Church's Christmas DVD entitled *Joy To The World*. I stood up and reminded them all that the Spirit of Christmas was really the Spirit of Christ. I told them that amidst all of our efforts in Iraq away from family and loved ones, that according to the degree to which we remember Christ and all that He represents to us, our hearts would be filled with a greater sense of connection and peace.

I assured them that God would consecrate our efforts to defend freedom and build a new Iraq in freedom's light. I testified to everyone present that we were each instruments in God's hands, to hold our lamps high so that the light we let shine could be seen by all Iraqis and have an impact on their hearts for good. Then I showed a segment of President Gordon B. Hinckley testifying to the world of the Living Christ, His divine birth and life, death and resurrection.

The other leaders were silent, and I could tell that each Officer and Non-Commissioned Officer alike were deeply touched by the words of the Lord's living prophet as he testified of the Living Christ.

I concluded the meeting with a prayer. A special feeling of peace permeated the room, and I sensed that the Officers and Non-Commissioned Officers felt as I did. Christmas was upon us, and we were beginning to enjoy the Season regardless of our separation, or the duty calling us to sacrifice our personal comfort.

The timely DVD sent by the Church was a direct answer to my prayers. I had struggled with my Christmas message.

These two wonderful, courageous people are leaders in the Chaldean Catholic Church. The man is the Ambassador to Rome for that church. There are evidences of faith in God and a belief in Jesus Christ reemerging throughout Iraq.

Sadly, there will still be many struggles in Iraq. These eight soldiers that are being memorialized were on patrol when they were killed by a car bomb that also wounded several other soldiers.

This photo shows the line to the Iraqi Pay Site. This line went on for two miles. Thousands of Iraqi soldiers wanted to be paid, but we were only able to process and pay about 5,500 men each day.

One of the soldiers caught me taking a little nap.
Sometimes I had to snag a bit of sleep whenever I could.

Here's a hint at American life creeping into Iraqi society.
I enjoyed this sign at a local food stand.

This lady's smiling face symbolizes the new hope that has come into the lives of many Iraqis. It has been a difficult transition, but there is a feeling that better days are ahead for the Iraqi people.

I couldn't decide on what to do, or how to do it. I wanted to provide a worship service that would be memorable and have a lasting impact on the lives of those that would be present.

Being in a combat zone does have its limitations. After much thought and some prayer, I had determined that a service focusing on the resurrected Christ would have greater impact than simply focusing on His birth. Christmas is the season of celebrating the birth of Christ, and every chaplain in Iraq was spending a lot of time and effort in making Christ's birth, along with Santa Claus, the center of the occasion.

Somehow, the thought of Christmas not having much value without Easter made a lot of sense, and sharing my testimony of the Living Christ while celebrating His birth felt right. My problem, with my limited resources, was putting a program together that would have the memorable impact I wanted to create. Music resources were limited, and talent was scarce, since our defensive posture had increased due to intelligence reports of possible attacks.

During my planning and preparation for the service, however, I never felt completely good about my final product. So, back to planning and rewriting the Christmas program. I have to admit that up until Christmas Eve day, I struggled with putting my worship service together.

As I said, the arrival of *Joy to the World* DVD was an answer to prayer. I spent the majority of Christmas Eve day reworking the arrangement of my worship service and organizing what I was going to say.

The sky began to grow gray in the late afternoon, and the air was quiet. There were no helicopters or sounds of Bradley Fighting Vehicles (track vehicles that make a lot of noise when they ride along paved streets).

By 7 p.m., I worked my way to the location where I would hold my worship service, a theater located at the former Ba'ath Party Headquarters. I set everything up for the service and miraculously had everything I needed—a projector, laptop computer and sound system, plus a large screen and plenty of candles.

At one point I had to stop and take everything in. Here I was, separated from my family, miles from home in a foreign land, yet getting ready to hold a Christmas Worship service. I had everything I needed to share the DVD and the wonderful message of the Living Christ.

The appointed time for the service finally came, and soldiers and commanders entered the theater. I watched as a battalion commander stood before his soldiers and welcomed everyone to worship along with him in remembering the special event of the Christ Child's birth. The battalion's Command Sergeant Major also participated by playing his guitar and singing "O Little Town of Bethlehem."

As we watched the DVD with images of the Church's Conference Center, the Tabernacle Choir, and the lighted spires of the Salt Lake Temple, my heart was filled with tremendous gratitude. I knew that although I was separated from my own family, I was experiencing and witnessing marvelous things happening before my eyes in a place where soldiers had been killed within the last 24 hours. Suddenly, the pain of separation was not at the forefront of my thoughts and feelings. Instead, I was filled with love and warmth, with gratitude for the Lord's atoning sacrifice.

Near the end of the service, I invited everyone to light the candle provided for them, and we dimmed the lights. In the light of the candles, I quoted the following verse:

> Ye are the light of the world. A city that is set on an hill cannot be hid.

Neither do men light a candle, and put it under a bushel, but on a candlestick; and it giveth light unto all that are in the house.

Let your light so shine before men, that they may see your good works, and glorify your Father which is in heaven.
—Matthew 5:14-16

There was a peaceful spirit in that theater. I looked down upon each soldier there and could tell they were being fed spiritually.

Somehow, looking up at that beautiful crescent moon with that bright star shining above it on Christmas night, I could not help but think how wonderfully blessed I had been that Christmas in Baghdad in 2003.

Rather than the pain of separation, I felt peace and calm. I knew I was experiencing sorrow, pain and hardship, but was not having to suffer from it all. The Lord had provided me with sufficient peace and comfort to manage my emotions and continue to focus on my purpose and mission to the soldiers I served with. I was amazed at how generous the Lord was in giving me such peace amidst the conflict requiring my presence in Iraq.

I marveled that I was allowed to experience a bit of history, feeling more connected than ever with the past, as I gazed up at that bright lone star, similar to that new star in the heavens that led men to Christ anciently, this star was leading me now. In my heart, I was very much connected to and enjoying my moment with the Lord of Hosts.

I could not stop the tears from flowing as I pondered my great blessings. I knew as I stood gazing up at that moon and star that Jesus is indeed the Christ, and that He actually does live, and loves me and everyone else. The tears of gratitude erased any feelings or thoughts of loneliness or depression from being separated from my wife and children. I was not alone nor was I forgotten, and in that moment, that was all that mattered.

As I walked back from the theater after the service with my commander and battalion executive officer, the sounds of war thundered in the distance. We could hear the "whuap, whuap" of the 105 mm howitzer fired from a AC-130 Gunship somewhere high in the air. Small arms fire cracked in the distance and as we walked together near midnight, not many words were spoken. Each was reflecting on the powerful spirit we felt earlier in the service.

I could tell that Christ and the blessings of His sacrifice had taken front stage in the hearts and minds of these good officers. We were surrounded by the sounds of war and combat, yet we walked in peace with the assuring comfort that God was watching us and protecting us. Almost as though we were being wrapped in the blanket of His great love, we didn't seem to notice that combat was actually being conducted around us.

Christmas Day began at 4:00 a.m., when we were all to "stand to." This is the term used to direct vigilance or be in a ready posture. "Stand to" means that everybody has to man or operate a defensive fighting position, and it is generally used to describe a period of time early in the morning before Early Morning Nautical Twilight (EMNT), or sunrise.

Intelligence reports had again indicated that dissident forces were going to attack in force. I grabbed my cell phone and walked out to one of our closest checkpoints. As I let each soldier call home, I assisted in manning their positions. By spending time with them at the checkpoint so early in the morning, I was able to get a feel for "how" the soldiers were. I assumed that they would all be miserable and angry for having to "stand to" so early, and for not being able to sleep in on this one special day of the year.

What I saw, however was completely different. Each soldier was physically cold, but their spirits were high and cheerful. They assumed their positions with professional haste, and did not utter a single complaint.

The sun arose, and in the new day's light everything was calm and still. It was very peaceful, and what a joy it was to spend those moments with young men willing to stand at the ready for the defense of our precious freedom.

Christmas Day was going to be special for the soldiers of the 40th Engineer Battalion. We had scheduled a football game between the officers and Non-Commissioned Officers. The sky was blue and the sun warmed everything and everyone. Christmas Day turned out to be a wonderful time together as a battalion. Unit morale was high and soldiers in the battalion seemed to have a greater peace and a brighter light about them.

Light is a marvelous thing, and we take it for granted. As I pondered the situation in Iraq, and our presence there, I couldn't help but remember a time in Japan during my mission when Gordon B. Hinckley spoke to the missionaries in my mission about the time clock of the Lord. I felt humbled that I was allowed to participate in the events shaping this country and preparing it for the restored gospel of the Lord Jesus Christ. I could sense the great pendulum of time shifting and bringing with it a change in the hearts of the people here in Iraq.

I could almost hear the anthems being sung by those angelic hosts as they sang praising God on that night of the Christ Child's birth, "Glory to God in the Highest, and on earth, peace good will toward men."

CHAPTER SEVEN
CONCLUDING THOUGHTS

> *Let us hear the conclusion of the whole matter: Fear God, and keep his commandments: for this is the whole duty of man.*
>
> —Ecclesiastes 12:13

Throughout our initial tour in Iraq, I would tell soldiers that the Lord has blessed my life with time away from family and loved ones to help me become a better husband, a better father, and a much better man. They would simply laugh and act as though I was on drugs. But I was persistent. When we were all but ready to redeploy, and received our extension, keeping us in the country another 90 to 120 days, I would say, "I guess the Lord really likes the progress I've been making because He wants me to do more of it."

How much more simple can it really be? In the final analysis, the conclusion of the whole matter will be summed up in our faithfulness, our loyalty, and our righteous attainment. We will either be one with the Lord, or separated from Him and His Holy Spirit.

In compiling my experiences and lessons learned, I have not attempted to make a definitive statement on any one issue, but rather have attempted to offer my thoughts and feelings that have come as a result of my experiences in hope that someone else might find something positive to relate to and in some way find encouragement and inspiration that will lead them to get on their knees and seek out divine guidance on their own.

The Prophet Joseph Smith's words provide me with instruction and peace at the same time, prompting me to act as he did to find the truth he was seeking.

> *At length I came to the conclusion that I must either remain in darkness and confusion, or else I must do as James directs, that is, ask of God. I at length came to the determination to "ask of God," concluding that if he gave wisdom to them that lacked wisdom, and would give liberally, and not upbraid, I might venture.*

—Joseph Smith History 1:13

AN ATTITUDE OF PRAYER

Prayer has been my immediate source of peace and comfort over the years, but especially while in a combat zone filled with danger at every turn. I would begin my day with a four-mile run along the Tigress River early in the morning as the sun would rise, and my heart would fill with gratitude for my life's many blessings. I could not hold back and run without prayer. Prayer that began as an expression of gratitude soon gave way to prayer expressing concern and heartfelt desires. More times than not, much of my prayer expressed my resolve and commitment to being who and what the Lord needed me to be for the soldiers around me. Most of my runs would be done in prayer.

This attitude of prayer would lead into a continuation of gratitude for breakfast, and would continue as I left to go out to be with my soldiers. I would continue my prayer even when counseling soldiers with their various issues, such as asking the Lord to allow me to see the person in front of me as He did, or to feel His great love for them, that I may also be filled with the love of God and of all men. (Mosiah 2:4)

Many times others have asked me, "So, who does the chaplain turn to when he needs counseling?" I almost find this question humorous, and want to laugh at it every time I hear it. I reply that I turn to my knees and seek God and His counsel. I have yet to find sufficient peace and comfort that can match that which comes from my Father in Heaven.

Many people view prayer as a single act, but I am learning to view prayer as an attribute and character trait which influences and determines our attitudes. Prayer as an act is nothing more than an expression, which could be one of pride and arrogance, or of humility and meek submission. Usually, I find that my attitude at any particular time will be reflected in the prayers I offer. Or perhaps, the prayers that I offer will be reflected in the attitude that I have at that moment.

Heaven only knows that I have offered my share of proud and arrogant prayers—those prayers where I do the telling and asking, with an air of expectation and demand.

How much differently would our lives be if we developed an attitude of prayer in which our entire thought processes and desires were mere extensions of this attitude?

President Ezra Taft Benson once stated:

> *Usually the Lord gives us the overall objectives to be accomplished and some guidelines to follow, but he expects us to work out most of the details and methods. The methods and procedures are usually developed through study and prayer and by living so that we can obtain and follow the promptings of the Spirit. Less spiritually advanced people, such as those in the days of Moses, had to be commanded in many things. Today those spiritually alert look at the objectives, check the guidelines laid down*

by the Lord and his prophets, and then prayerfully act—
without having to be commanded 'in all things.' This
attitude prepares men for godhood.
                  (*Conference Report*, April 1965, p. 121.)

As I read this for the first time, the words and phrases, "prayerfully act" and "this attitude prepares men for godhood" caught my immediate attention. If prayer was intended to be a single event or act, then once the prayer was completed, any action made would be independent of and separate from that prayer. But "prayerfully act" indicates an action along with and in connection to the prayer. This means to me that prayer is to become part of my behavior. Behavioral prayer must have emotional and mental foundations, which will influence attitude, desire and ultimately outward behavior.

Imagine the change that would take place in a person if prayer became a constant filter through which all thoughts and desires were to pass. We would eliminate and remove all doubt as to whether or not a single thought, a feeling, a desire, and even behavior would offend or invite the Holy Spirit in our lives.

We would be ever grounded in What Matters Most in our lives, living according to the enticings of the Holy Spirit, and becoming Saints, through the atonement of Christ the Lord.

The Lord has given me many opportunities and experiences by which I have learned that prayer is and should always be more than an act. It should also be an attitude in which we lose ourselves and become someone new and alive in the Spirit of the Lord. The prayer that we utter should become part of our very thought process, and provide us with the filter through which we clean our thoughts, and dedicate our behaviors and actions to Heavenly Father. It is through this very same process that we receive inspiration and spiritual guidance. The whisperings of the Still Small Voice have come to me as I have found myself caught up in this attitude of prayer. My greatest insights have occurred when I have given myself to this attitude of praying with my heart, mind and soul.

I can testify that this is not something that is easy to do at first. It requires practice, plus time to develop the mind and heart to have the flexibility and range of motion required to function in and with the spirit. This much like exercising our muscles and training ourselves for an athletic event.

On one afternoon, I had an opportunity to sit and discuss religion and life with an Iraqi woman named Shahanez, who lost her husband to Saddam's evil regime. This sweet little Muslim woman taught me more in a few minutes about Christianity than I have learned from many of the Christians I know.

During our discussion, she looked me in the eyes and said, "I am a Muslim, as you know, but I hate Islam and what it has become. Today, Islam in not real or true. True Islam means to love the God and all of the God's creation to include the earth. We Muslims must pray five times a day. People go to the mosque and say the same prayers over and over. I do not go to the mosque and pray. I know that the God sees into my heart, and knows my prayer to Him. I love my God too much, and I do not pray five times a day, or ask Him anything for me—just to never leave me—because I need my God in my life all the day. So I pray all the time, in my heart and in my mind. I love all of the God's messengers. Your Jesus is very dear in my heart. I always pray to the God. He knows my heart, and I am pure before Him."

I had to take a moment to let her words sink in and settle against my own feelings of needing and wanting my Father in Heaven's presence in my life.

One day the battalion commander was out making his various rounds in Baghdad. His convoy was attacked by a remote-controlled explosive device. No one was badly hurt, but it was clear to me and everyone in that convoy that divine intervention was in effect. Prayer and faith, combined with dedication to their duty, got them through the ordeal.

Later in the evening I got to speak to the group of soldiers involved in the incident. Looking at their faces and feeling the spirit of love the commander held for his soldiers, I was impressed that the Lord had a hand in their protection that day.

Prayer is so much more than an expression, It is a shield, and even a way of living and dealing with the opposition we face in life.

On another occasion, I was visiting the home of Janet Kassup. One of the women in her small community had been murdered in the middle of the night, and everyone struggled with fear and worry about their own families.

Janet was especially fearful and overcome by worry. The atmosphere of the entire community was dark and depressing. I walked into the Kassup home and they all seemed to perk up a bit, forcing smiles and acting gracious, but I could tell that they were not happy or comfortable with the conditions in their community. After a few moments of listening to them express their concerns and fears, I bore my testimony of the power of prayer, and then asked if they would like to have a family prayer.

Janet nodded affirmatively, so we all knelt down and

held hands. Then I began to pray. Ammar, the oldest son, translated my words as I prayed, and a special spirit of comfort and peace distilled down upon that home. I felt the heaviness of their hearts lighten, and when I finished the prayer, Janet's eyes were dripping wet from tears of gratitude. Ammar, too, was crying from the experience he just had with the Spirit.

I got up from that prayer with the feeling that something remarkable had just taken place, and it had. The Kassups now kneel together more often, and continue in what I had taught them about inviting the comforting presence of the Lord into their home amidst the chaos that surrounds them.

When I first arrived in Iraq, the battalion commander had me pray at the end of our first command and staff meeting. He said, "Chaplain, I need you to pray." So I did. That prayer set a precedent that every officer and NCO in that meeting grew to expect. I was soon being asked to pray at all of our official gatherings, including our officer physical fitness events.

On one occasion, the battalion commander could not make it, so the responsibility of the event fell on one of the company commanders. I participated in the athletic event, a game of combat soccer, and at the conclusion of the game, the Captain gathered everyone together as the battalion commander did, and he gave words of encouragement and guidance. Then he turned to me and said, "Chaplain, we're not finished until you give us a prayer."

I was impressed at how that group of officers had developed an attitude of prayer, however small it may have been. It was an attitude all the same, and they expected it to happen.

One week, I missed the command and staff meeting

because of an emergency. The following week, the battalion commander got up and asked me to pray, emphasizing that he really needed me to pray with his commanders and first sergeants. It humbled me to have a commander tell me that I needed to pray more with them and for them. Now if I can only help them all develop this attitude to include personal and private prayers in their lives.

I have gained a strong testimony of prayer, and that the scriptures are correct! Things always do work out for my good when I simply lose myself in my search and prayer for truth.

> *Search diligently, pray always, and be believing, and all things shall work together for your good, if ye walk uprightly and remember the covenant wherewith ye have covenanted one with another.*
> —Doctrine and Covenants 90:24

The thought struck me one day concerning "believing." I can't help but think that this word has perhaps a much deeper meaning than we normally attach to it. "Be" is a verb indicating the action of "who" I am, and "lieving" is a version of the phrase "to live," indicating the action of "becoming."

Therefore, my believing is really a description of "who I am, or am becoming." Or simply put, my "belief" is really a statement of my "being" and "living." To say I "believe in Jesus Christ" is to say "I am becoming like Jesus Christ."

Isn't it interesting that prayer funnels our thoughts and emotions to align them with the Savior? To say that I believe, and therefore pray, is to really say that I am becoming and actively working on thinking and feeling as He does, making my belief more complete.

I sometimes visited the home of a widowed Iraqi woman and her four daughters. This small family had been blacklisted by the local Iraqis because her husband had been executed by Saddam Hussein in 1999. With no job or other means of supporting themselves, they struggled to get by.

I began bringing them food, clothing and medical supplies sent to me by people in the United States. On one occasion, this woman tearfully told me that she was ashamed at the Muslims in her own country. They had abandoned her and her children, going against the tenants of Islam about caring for the poor and needy. She felt embarrassed to be receiving so much care and attention from an American soldier.

I assured her that God was aware of her and had heard her prayers. I told her I was there to be part of His answer to her. God loved her, and was pleased with her choices to live correctly and righteously. She had worked hard at teaching her daughters to be upright and morally clean young women. She had taught them to pray individually and as a family. Most importantly, she had taught them to love God and to submit themselves to His will for them.

THE GREATEST DECEPTION OF ALL

One issue I have learned to take great opposition to is that of anything regarding the "self." Self-esteem, self-worth, self-confidence, self-control, and so on. I have watched men in the heat of battle and its bloody aftermath lose all self-confidence.

These were men that went into the conflict with seemingly high esteem, confidence and worth of "self." But the rigorous and violent demands of the battlefield stripped them of their sense of "self."

Beyond "self" they had nothing to turn to but God and whatever small shred of hope and faith that they could muster. Often times they relied on the chaplains or other men they esteem and admire to boost their own faith and confidence to survive and endure the difficulty of combat.

I have determined, and believe with all my heart, that the adversary does not want us to see the truth of the whole matter. Satan wants each of us to grow content with ourselves, trusting in and relying on our own devices. Satan wants us to exclude God and His plan for happiness.

My father-in-law taught me this principle when I married his daughter more than two decades ago. He approached me, putting his arm around my shoulder and said with a big smile, "Now Tony, we're glad you have married our daughter, but we want you to learn to love the Lord more than you love Jeaneice."

I have to admit, I thought this to be the stupidest thing I had ever heard! (Not to mention the most unromantic advice.) Why would a father instruct a son-in-law to love God more than their own daughter?

Over the years however, I have found that his advice was not only the most correct, but also the most important for me to truly find happiness and joy with his daughter.

After a recent attack on a convoy, a young Captain in Iraq broke down and wept heavily as he realized that he alone did not amount to much. He sensed he was meandering along without much more purpose than what the Army provided for him. The realization that his command did not equate to who he really was shook him deeply.

Before the attack on his convoy and the loss of one of his soldiers, he saw himself as confident and completely in control of his life and circumstances. His position as commander fed his esteem and pumped him with arrogant confidence.

Suddenly, the loss of a soldier shook the foundation of his esteem and confidence. He found himself suddenly short and didn't know where to turn for comfort and peace.

My experiences have taught me that there is only one source sufficient to supply all of us with the esteem and confidence necessary to weather the storms of life. This source is vital, whether on the battlefield or in the safety of our own homes where complacency and boredom can become as menacing as an opposing force bent on killing us. I have learned that the purpose of having a "greatest commandment in the law" (Matt 22:34-40) is to help each of us prevent moments of worldly sorrow and devastation.

By learning to "give" our hearts, minds and souls to the Lord first, in the attitude of love, we will truly learn how to love ourselves. Not with a "self-love" but with the love of God and of all men. (Mosiah 2:4) There is no other way in which we can truly learn to love our neighbor as ourselves.

I have learned that self-esteem, self-worth and all other forms of "self" indulgence feed our natural tendencies and cloud our minds from really seeing the truth of our existence here on earth. We are here to have joy. This is the reason Adam fell, that you and I may have joy, which only comes from living and being worthy to receive the Spirit of the Lord. All we need to receive the Spirit of the Lord is to love Him, which will lead us to obey Him, which allows us to see as He sees things, and then experience life as He does.

Perception really is everything! And the Borgs from the Delta Quadrant (*Star Trek: The Next Generation*) have it right when they say, "Resistance is futile!"

To perceive "self" as being important, then all of the worldly struggles that are required to maintain the image of "self" will become our daily battlefield. I have spent a fair amount of my time on that field of battle, and have learned that "self" is not sufficient to conquer, or even to survive. In the final analysis, "self" will have to bow before the Master and account for resisting and neglecting Him and His plan for our happiness and peace, which plan has no room for "self."

Satan desires our misery and discontent. He wishes every one of us walking this earth to be miserable like unto himself. He has craftily devised a program, tested and tried throughout the ages, that blinds our minds and hearts against God and His plan for our happiness. It is not a complicated or sophisticated plan. All it requires is a simple deception—a slight skewing of the truth—leaving most of the truth intact at first glance. But this deception increases and grows with time and distance. What percentage of truth is required for truth to be truth?

100 percent!

My respect for Satan's title, "the father of all lies" has deepened and grown, as I have witnessed firsthand how dark and blind the hearts of many I have worked with have become. I have recognized within myself just how powerful the adversary's deception program really is. I have found that I have fallen short on many occasions and have been responsible for the separation between the Lord and myself.

There is no BIG lie, or GREAT deception, there are only small and minor lies and deceptions. We turn them into the big and great lies and deceptions that they ultimately become as we cling to them and resist the Light of Christ and the enticings of the Holy Spirit.

Satan sits at our waypoints, trying to slightly nudge us from the intended course, knowing that our misguided path will be nearly unnoticeable at first. But in the forests and jungles of life, and amidst the storms that prevail, we will ultimately become lost and disconnected from our objective.

When I arrived in Iraq, I was impressed with the size and magnitude of many of the former regime's buildings. The palaces and headquarters buildings were magnificent structures. From a distance, the workmanship and appearance of the buildings seemed incredibly fine and very impressive. One day I got to walk around the very large Ba'ath Party Headquarters building, which was perhaps three-quarters completed before we bombed it for the second time in ten years. The construction and workmanship was the worst I had even seen! There weren't any straight lines or true angles anywhere. Everything on the inside was merely thrown together and bound by a lot of cement and steel to hold it together. The materials were substandard and absolutely looked terrible. My first impression walking through the building was, "How could such a large and magnificent structure be so shabbily and poorly constructed?"

On the outside, however, the building looked first class, with sharp corners and stunning designs. Everything was covered in marble or stone, and the appearance was superb.

I began to think just how much we sometimes let ourselves become like that building. On the inside we are poorly constructed and held together with false hopes, groundless faith, and arrogant self-pride. All of our energy and effort is spent on making our façade—the outside—look right, proper, and true.

I have learned in the combat zone of Iraq that when my focus is on "self" then I cannot be focused on the Lord! Self is a master demanding attention and submissive devotion. Self is jealous and defensive, quick and eager to exclude any notion of God and His plan for my happiness. Self makes light of Christ's light within each of us, and diminishes any promptings and enticings of the Holy Spirit. Self is that "mammon" the Lord spoke of, warning us of the dangers of becoming deceived and led astray by the blindness and hardness of our hearts.

> No man can serve two masters: for either he will hate the one, and love the other; or else he will hold to the one, and despise the other. Ye cannot serve God and mammon.
> —Matthew 6:24

In the instant I focus on "self" I divide myself and become torn and separated from the presence of the Lord. In that same instant, I create conflict within my life. The only acceptable solution for the sudden conflict is to preserve the image of "self." This is done at the expense of those around me, including those I love and revere. They become, in my blinded condition, the culprits and designers of my misery. The truth, however, is that I am the culprit and designer of the misery I experience. It was my choice to focus on "self" that separated me from the presence of the Lord in the first place.

The scary thing is that this dynamic occurs multiple times each day, and at varying degrees. Most of the time it slips by unnoticed and unchecked, increasing the gap between the truth of how I am and how the Lord wants me to be.

Unfortunately for most of us, it takes a moment of extreme hardship or sorrow to make us face the truth of our situation. For many of the American soldiers in Iraq, that realization took place in the face of danger and death.

I put my arm around one such soldier and held him as he wept at the sudden and stark realization that without God, he was nothing. This realization erased his notion that "self" was all he needed. We spoke of the importance of thinking about and living for God. The faint and flickering light within him began to illuminate his understanding. Combined with his experience that shook him to the very core, he began to change. A week later, I almost didn't recognize this young soldier, as his face radiated with the light of desire to live for the Lord, and be who God wanted him to be: honest, faithful, and true in every way. My new rule of thumb has become, "Anytime that 'self' applies, then the solution is only temporary at best. The permanent solution can only exist when I sacrifice 'self' and live for the Lord."

PEACE BE STILL

How different would the lives be of those husbands and wives that experience geographical separation because of deployment, business, or any other circumstances, if they remained steadfast and unmovable in their relationship with the Lord?

They would still be subject to the hardships and difficulties that accompany separation, but they would do so with greater inner peace. They would be able to stand strong against anything that came against them, giving them the strength and courage to press forward.

Also, they would find that they are not alone. They are accompanied by the Lord, who has already traveled down the trail of great tears and sorrow, and who knows in intimate detail how to give comfort and peace. We will notice that our spouses will be by our side, encouraging and lending strength and support, rather than betraying and deserting us in our times of greatest need.

Nephi's counsel on this is very clear, and it lends insight into helping each of us to be more determined and resolved in being true to ourselves and to the testimonies we each have. Being true ultimately changes us into the people that will stand with great confidence in the presence of the Lord and His hosts.

> *Wherefore, ye must press forward with a steadfastness in Christ, having a perfect brightness of hope, and a love of God and of all men. Wherefore, if ye shall press forward, feasting upon the word of Christ, and endure to the end, behold, thus saith the Father: Ye shall have eternal life.*
>
> *And now, behold, my beloved brethren, this is the way; and there is none other way nor name given under heaven whereby man can be saved in the kingdom of God. And now, behold, this is the doctrine of Christ, and the only and true doctrine of the Father, and of the Son, and of the Holy Ghost, which is one God, without end. Amen.*
> —2 Nephi 31:20-21

One day while I was preparing to conduct a worship service in Baghdad, I pondered on what I might say to lend inspiration and strength to those that would attend. My soldiers were tired and growing more and more hardened from the violence and stress that surrounded them.

I was reading again about the storm-tossed sea, and the terrified disciples who struggled for peace and assurance. I had spoken about this story before, attempting to encourage my soldiers to take strength and courage in knowing that the Lord would calm all of their storms, and that He would make their seas calm and the prevailing wind to be still.

A thought struck me, however, that made me rethink that story, and the hardship and difficulty we experienced in abundance each day in Iraq. I was bothered by the rebuke the Savior gave to His disciples after He calmed the sea.

> *And when they had sent away the multitude, they took him even as he was in the ship. And there were also with him other little ships.*

And there arose a great storm of wind, and the waves beat into the ship, so that it was now full.

And he was in the hinder part of the ship, asleep on a pillow: and they awake him, and say unto him, Master, carest thou not that we perish?

And he arose, and rebuked the wind, and said unto the sea, Peace, be still. And the wind ceased, and there was a great calm.

And he said unto them, Why are ye so fearful? how is it that ye have no faith?

And they feared exceedingly, and said one to another, What manner of man is this, that even the wind and the sea obey him?

—Mark 4:36-41

I had always wondered about this rebuke. How could it be that the disciples had no faith when they turned to the Lord to get Him to fix their dire circumstance? Was that not a demonstration of faith, however simple it may be?

These were seasoned men of the sea, and knew it well. They knew how to weather a storm. Perhaps, having grown up on this very sea, these men had seen storms come and go, but had never seen a storm of this magnitude so suddenly appear, threatening to consume everything on the water. After a period of time that allowed the boat to nearly be filled with water, these hardened fishermen turned to the Lord, waking Him and asking Him if He didn't care that they were soon going to perish.

The thought that grabbed me was this: "How much differently would that story have been if those fishermen, the chosen disciples of the Lord, simply grabbed the ropes and railing available, and silently resolved to hold on and ride the storm out, as the Son of the Living God lay peacefully asleep in the hinder part of their ship?" The Christ, their Master, remained asleep, undisturbed by the wind and water. So why should they be disturbed?

Suddenly, my mind raced searching all of the stories and scriptures I knew of that spoke of faith and belief in God. I realized that this was the only instance I could find where the Lord chastised His disciples regarding their lack of faith in the midst of extreme difficulty. The Savior continued to teach them and help them understand the principle of faith following this event, but every one of those aboard that boat that stormy night had learned one important lesson—that in all of our boats, the Lord lays fast asleep. He sleeps because He is not afraid, nor is he concerned about the temporal aspects of the storm. Only we humans, in our narrow outlook on life, worry about such temporary things. The fact that He is there with each of us should be enough. There are times, however, when we, like those early disciples, choose to run and wake Him to save us from our fears and uncertain difficulties.

When life's storms rock our security, threatening to destroy, we have only to look to the hinder part of our ships and be assured that He is there. The prophet Joseph Smith taught that faith is assurance.

As we exercise our faith, we become faithful, and in this newly found attribute, of faithfulness, we find assurance, and in this assurance, we find comfort, peace and joy.

This is one more direct benefit of prayer. The more Spirit- directed our prayers are, the more certain we can be that He is with us. To wake Him and want Him to calm the storm is to forfeit our roles and the purpose of life's storms, which teach us to have resolve and be at peace, filled with inner calm amidst the storms, trusting completely in Him.

Each of those disciples lived lives filled with hardship,

sorrow, and uncertainty. Each of them fell into the hands of murderous men. Each fulfilled faithfully their assigned stewardships, holding on firmly to the ropes and railing, with the assurance that the Lord was with them always.

To study their individual lives, it becomes very apparent that they each rode out the storms, silently and with great inner resolve to hold on tightly, so as to not disturb the sleeping Savior in the hindermost part of their boats.

How different would marriages be if husbands and wives would simply grab hold of the ropes and railing available and ride the storms out with the inner resolve to express their faith by being faithful as opposed to being fearful, or doubting?

I could not help but think of this story of the Lord calming the sea and stilling the wind, as I read the message from the wife concerned about her husband's attitude. As she looked for an immediate fix, or for someone else to calm her fears, I realized the only true solution to her problem was to develop that inner resolve to simply grab hold of the ropes, hang on, and ride the storm out. This is the demonstration of real faith, and in this way we are demonstrating our faithfulness to each other, and our real love for the Lord.

It is in these moments of real difficulty that our brightest light can be seen, if we are faithfully holding on and steadfastly pressing forward in Christ. To be of real worth to the Lord's effort in bringing the gospel's message of love and peace to all that will listen, we must be anchored securely and firmly to the sure foundation which is, has always been and will ever continue to be Jesus Christ.

Separation may happen to us either physically or geographically, but never let it happen to us spiritually. How grateful I am for the Holy Scriptures that instruct and edify me, and for the Prophets that have sacrificed greatly to provide me with the knowledge I need to truly understand what my Father in Heaven needs me to be.

I have shared but a small part of my experiences in Iraq. There are many more things that I am still pondering for the lessons yet to be learned. I am grateful for the true and everlasting gospel of Jesus Christ! It has truly been one of the most memorable and remarkable events of my life to be in Iraq, a country that has been without the priesthood of God for thousands of years. What an honor it has been to participate in a sacrament service, or listen to the humble testimonies of saints of God living and struggling to become who the Lord wants them to be.

I am grateful for hardship and difficulty, and for the lessons, the Lord has provided me. I am more intensely aware and critical of my actual position and progress towards the presence of my Father in Heaven.

This war has changed me, and will ever be a mark in my life directing me to be more, give more and live more for the Lord, that I may simply walk in His light and Spirit.

I have grown to love the Iraqi people. I have seen the characteristics of Father Abraham in many of them, and I have felt the great spirit of the Lord working among them. They are being prepared for the restored gospel of Jesus Christ and to bring many of them back into the fold of God. I am grateful that the Lord has allowed me to participate in such a grand event—an entire nation and people being prepared to receive and accept God's only Begotten Son.

I hope the stories I have shared will help someone find application and understanding to live a better life. I have learned through experience that the Lord indeed does love us and cares deeply about our happiness.

When asked, "Why are you always so happy, or positive, or upbeat?" I want to always be able to answer, "I know not, save the Lord commanded me to be."

The plan is so very simple. All it requires from us is resolve, and commitment. Physically living in the presence of the Lord someday will require that we become godly people, so we must learn to spiritually live in His presence today. We can begin becoming godly now, in this life, preparing our minds and hearts to seek righteousness continually.

ABOUT THE AUTHOR

Chaplain Anthony W. Horton served in Iraq with the 40th Engineer Battalion, 2nd Brigade Combat Team, 1st Armor Division for nearly one year. He received a phone call in May of 2003, while assigned to the 1st Military Intelligence Battalion in Wiesbaden, Germany, and was told to pack his bags. He was being reassigned to a unit that had just deployed to Iraq, and the unit needed a chaplain.

With bags already packed and waiting to deploy with the 1st MI, he took his orders and got on an Air Force plane straight to Baghdad International Airport, and began his most memorable adventure to date, serving and ministering to American soldiers and people of Baghdad.

Suddenly living in the ancient and historically rich land of Iraq, he began to study Abraham's journey from southern Iraq, in the land of the Chaldeans all the way to the Valley of Haran. He met Iraqis that claimed ancestral lineage to the ancient Chaldeans and Assyrians.

One particular group he became familiar with was a group of people claiming to be the original Iraqis, a remnant of those ancient people of Ur, the same people that Abraham came from. This particular group calls themselves the Mandaeans, and currently practice the religion they believe was handed down from Adam to Abraham to John the Baptist.

Chaplain Horton worked with several Muslim Imams and their families, discussing religion and God's plan of happiness for all of His children. In some of the communities in which Chaplain Horton worked, he became close friends with the people, being invited into their homes to eat from their tables, or floor, whichever was available.

Chaplain Horton served as an Army chaplain within the Green Zone in central Baghdad, but also was set apart by the Arabian Peninsula Stake President in Kuwait, to serve as the 13th member of that High Council for reporting and ecclesiastical accountability. While organizing Servicemen's Groups and helping to lead soldiers in weekly sacrament services—not to mention the many hours spent providing counsel and advice for his soldiers—Chaplain Horton was able to meet and assist many U.S. soldiers from the various units stationed in Iraq.

This book is the culmination of many of the rich experiences he had while serving in Iraq and the experiences of those he worked with there.

It is the author's intent to share his stories and experiences in Iraq with others in hopes that a better understanding of what conditions actually exist in Iraq and what struggles the Iraqi people have had to endure. He also shares his experiences in hopes that others may also share in the lessons he learned, as he ministered to soldiers and the Iraqi people alike.

DEC 42:14

MATT 5:38-39

LUKE 9:42